Schwerin

The Lakeside City

With contributions by
Ingrid Möller
Horst Ende
Ludwig Seyfarth

Translated by Helmut P. Einfalt

With photographs by
Angelika Heim
Hartmut Musewald
Andreas Peeck
Olaf Scherer

Edition Temmen

Die Deutsche Bibliothek – CIP-Einheitsaufnahme
Schwerin : the lakeside city / with contributions by Ingrid Möller …
Transl. by Helmut P. Einfalt. With photogr. by Angelika Heim …
[Ed.: Daniela Müller]. –
1. engl. ed. based upon the revised 5th German ed. –
Bremen : Ed. Temmen, 1995
Dt. Ausg. u.d.T.: Schwerin
ISBN 3-86108-423-6

NE: Möller, Ingrid; Heim, Angelika; Müller, Daniela [Red.]

Cover photograph:
Editor: Daniela Müller

Images by:
Angelika Heim: S. 54, 62, 67, 75, 78, 79, 83, 93, 98, 99, 100
Deutsche Luftbild: S. 86f.
Historisches Museum Schwerin: S. 72, 90
Hartmut Musewald: S. 4, 9, 34, 38f., 53, 55, 57,
59, 61, 64f., 71, 76f., 84, 91, 95, 96
Mecklenburg. Volkskundemuseum – Freilichtmuseum Schwerin-Muess: S. 29
Mecklenburgische Landesbibliothek: S. 16
Andreas Peeck: S. 37, 45, 82, 92
Olaf Scherer: S. 35, 47, 50f.
Staatliches Museum Schwerin: S. 42, 68, 69
Weisse Flotte, Hamburg: S. 63
Publishers' archives: S. 15, 19, 21, 23, 25, 26, 27, 31, 41, 43, 73, 89

First English edition based upon
the revised 5th German edtion.

© Edition Temmen
Hohenlohestr. 21 — 28209 Bremen
Tel. 0421-344280/341727 Fax: 0421-348094
All rights reserved.
Production: Edition Temmen
ISBN 3-86108-423-6

Table of Contents

Historical Survey

around 500 AD	Mecklenburg is colonized by Slavic tribes.
1018	In his chronicle, Thitmar von Merseburg first mentions Schwerin as »*Zuarin*«.
1160	*Zuarin* castle is taken by the Saxon duke *Heinrich der Löwe* (Henry the Lion). Victory over the *Obotrite* tribe. The Obotrite leader Niklot dies when attacking from Werle castle. Henry founds the city of Schwerin and names Gunzelin von Hagen as his first governor.
1167	Transfer of the bishop's see from *Mecklenburg* castle (south of *Wismar*) to Schwerin.
1171	The city is granted market rights. Consecration of the first cathedral.
Around 1190	Beginning of the construction work at the second cathedral.
1228	Constitution of Schwerin's City Council with six counsellors and one mayor

1270–1416	Construction of today's ogival cathedral.
1340	The city wall is finished.
1348	Emperor Charles IV institutes the dukedom of Mecklenburg
1358	After the death of the last count of Schwerin, Duke Albrecht II buys the City of Schwerin for 20,000 marks in silver and moves the dukal residency from *Wismar* to the »Fortress Schwerin«.
Around 1500	Schwerin has some 2,500 inhabitants excluding the *Schelfstadt* area.
1549	Beginning of the Lutheran Reformation in Mecklenburg.
1531–1679	Several fires destroy the medieval centre.
1553	Construction of the »Grand New House« at the Castle with terracotta ornaments by Statius von Düren.
1628–31	The dukes are expelled from Mecklenburg during the Thirty Years' War. *Wallenstein* becomes duke of Mecklenburg and takes his residency at *Güstrow*.
1701	The *Hofschauspielgesellschaft* [Court Acting Society] etablishes the first permanent theatre.
1705	Construction of the baroque New City on the *Schelfe*.
1752–1756	Construction of the *Schlossgarten* [Castle Gardens].
1753	Founding of the first German Theatre Academy by Konrad Ekhof.
1756–1837	Step by step, the residency is transferred to *Ludwigslust*.
1764	Schwerin now has 3288 inhabitants.
1815	At the Vienna Congress, the dukedoms of Mecklenburg-Schwerin and Mecklenburg-Strelitz are transformed into a Grand-Dukedom.
1819	The population has grown to 9,986 inhabitants.
1823	Georg Adolph Demmler (1804–86) becomes the dukal court architect.
1830	During the *Schweriner Münzaufstand* [Schwerin Coins Upheaval], craft masters, craftsmen and labourers fight for better living conditions..
1832	The Old Centre and the *Schelfstadt* are united.
1837	Grand Duke Paul Friedrich moves his residency back to Schwerin and has the old castle thoroughly refurbished.

After 1840	The city is extended towards the north-west to plans by Demmler, the *Pfaffenteich* area being included.
1842	The *Paulsdamm* dam across Lake Schwerin is finished.
1845–57	The Castle is refurbished according to G.A. Demmler's plans.
1847	Schwerin is linked to the Berlin-Hamburg railway line.
1848/49	The revolution does away with the old corporate constitution and establishes a liberal constitution granting the freedom of press, of gathering and of associations.
1851	In the course of political restoration, G.A Demmler is dismissed from his post as court architect because of his democratic attitude.
1857	Ceremonial inauguration of the New Castle on May 26.
1860	Schwerin has grown to 22,516 inhabitants.
1869	First appearance of the Social-Democratic Labour Party in Schwerin.
1886	The neo-baroque Court Theatre at the *Alter Garten* [Old Garden] is openeded.
1892	The construction of the cathedral spire is finished. The spire was designed by the architect Georg Daniel and measures 117.5 metres in height.
1918	Grand Duke Friedrich Franz IV resigns.
1920	Severe battles against the *Kapp-Putsch* [a right-wing putsch attempt organized by former army officers under the leadership of one Mr. Kapp].
1921–45	Several historical rooms at the castle are made accessible to the public.
1932	Schwerin now has 53,621 inhabitants. At the State Council elections, the *NSDAP* Nazi party wins a majority.
1938	The synagogue at *Schlachtermarkt* is destroyed during the anti-Jewish riots in the so-called »*Reichskristallnacht*« night from November 9 to 10.
1945	On May 2, U.S. troops reach the city. After the withdrawal of the Western allies under the Yalta treaty, Soviet troops occupy Mecklenburg and enter the city on July 1.

1952	Administrative reforms divide Mecklenburg into the districts of *Rostock, Schwerin,* and *Neubrandenburg.* Schwerin becomes district capital.
1955	Construction of the Western City between *Lübecker* and *Wittenburger Strasse* roads begins.
1962–72	The *Lankow* housing area is under development.
1971	Approval of the development plans and beginning of construction activities for the *Grosser Dreesch* area.
1972	With some 100,000 inhabitants, Schwerin is already a large city.
1977	Parts of the Old City at the *Grosser Moor* [Great Moor] are torn down and replaced by new constructions.
1982	Schwerin has 125,000 inhabitants.
1985	Celebration of Schwerin's 825th anniversary.
1989	On October 23, Schwerin sees its first Monday Demonstration at *Alter Garten* with some 40,000 participants.
1990	In the first free elections for the City Council on May 6, Johannes Kwaschik of the Social-Democratic party is elected Mayor. On October 27, 1990, the State Council of *Mecklenburg-Vorpommern* declares Schwerin State Capital.
1992	In the cours of a booming city development, new residential quarters, office buildings, supermarkets, hotels, and shopping centres, such as *Margarethenhof,* are built on the city's outskirts.
1993	April 28 sees a solemn farewell-ceremony for the last G.U.S. troops. On May 23, the Mecklenburg State Constituion (written in both German and Low German) becomes effective.
1995	Schwerin is one of the centres for the celebration of the »Mecklenburg Millenary«.

From The History Of Schwerin

A while ago I overheard a conversation between a girl of about four and her mother, when the girl asked: »And when did they invent this city?«. I listened in surprise. I could not understand the mother's answer, but her embarrassment was obvious.

So, what could the answer be? In the schoolbooks they say »The City of Schwerin was founded by Henry the Lion in 1160«. Such phrases had to be known by heart in former times. But how poor are their contents, after all! Now, the answer »Henry the Lion« would not be quite correct, for there had been settlements in today's city area a long time before him. The basic prerequisite for settlements are suitable geographical conditions. And if Fritz Reuter [a Mecklenburg author writing mostly in Low German, 1810–1874] says in his »*Urgeschicht von Meckelborg*« [Mecklenburg History Book] that the founders of Schwerin were »*de Poggen*«, i.e. the frogs, he comes quite close to the truth as this area was not only full of lakes, but also of woods, swamps and moors. In the middle Stone Age (10,000 to 3,000 BC) hunters roved through this area, and from 3000 B.C., early peasants who settled here left their traces as did their successors in the Bronze and Iron Ages. Flint knives and arrowheads, ceramic fragments and jewellery – much of what was left behind by them has found its way into Schwerin's *Museum für Ur- und Frühgeschichte* [Museum of Pre- and Early History]. There, we also find the remainders of the later Germanic settlers, when there was extensive trade and first contacts with the Romans. Various tribes entered the area and left it again. Around 500 AD, Slavic tribes colonized the scarcely populated area. Among the castles they built in the course of the next centuries we find the *Michelenburg* at *Dorf Mecklenburg* that later gave its name to the whole country, and *Zuarin* castle (i.e. Schwerin), which means »area full of animals and woods«.

The Founding Of Schwerin

The earliest description of such a castle in a lake – although nothing proves that Schwerin is referred to in that statement – dates back to 973. In Arabic letters, Ibrahim Ibm Jakub writes about the Slavs:

»Whenever they want to build a castle they select a grassy ground rich in water, weeds and swamps. They stake a building site, dig a moat and heap up the dug-out soil, which is then stamped down. A wall is erected to the necessary height, a gate and a bridge over the moat are built. Enemy troops can enter the land of Nakon only with difficulty, for it consists of meadows, swamps, and moors.«

Whoever wants to get an impression of this situation should go to the *Archäologisches Freilichtmuseum* [Archeological Open-Air Museum] at *Gross Raden* near *Sternberg*, where such a Slavic fortification with a temple and a wall has been reconstructed in full size.

The earliest document which names *Zuarin* Castle is the chronicle of Bishop Thietmar of Merseburg, dated 1018. The chronicler writes that the Liutite tribe settling in the East had conquered the castle of Mistislav the Obotrite. One generation later, however, the castle is back in Obotrite hands.

In the course of the Eastern expansion of the German feudal Lords, the country of the Slavs is conquered by the Saxon duke Henry the Lion. In 1147, the participants in a crusade against the *Sorbs* (a Slavic tribe) meet powerful resistance. Only in the summer of 1160, Henry and his huge army – with Danish support from the coast – can achieve a decision in his favour.

In view of the superior force of the enemy, the Obotrite defenders give up the fortification and move back to the countryside. Their leader Niklot dies in the fight for *Werle* castle near *Schwaan*.

In the same year, Henry the Lion had the strategically placed fortress rebuilt and founded a city at the same place. He granted the settlement all the rights of a city, his own seal – a rider on horse-back with a shield – serves as the city's arms to the present day. Henry appointed Gunzelin von Hagen from Brunswick as his governor. The small German settlement was situated in today's Market area. The Sorbs who had been living in the castle area gradually moved to the »shelf« areas. Their share of the population must have been quite high, for in 1167 Henry saw himself forced to call Pribislav, Niklot's son as the latter's heir. Thus, a Sorb prince became the ancestor of the Mecklenburg princes! Gunzelin von Hagen was named the first Count of Schwerin.

With the Cistercian Berno, Schwerin got its first bishop. Being the centre of both a bishopric and a county were to determine the city life for many centuries to come. In 1171, the first cathedral was consecrated. After Count Henry I of Schwerin had brought along the relic of the Holy Blood from a pilgrimage to the Holy Land in 1222, the city became a place of pilgrimage. Soon, the cathedral was too small for all the pilgrims, therefore it was rebuilt in 1248 and 1270. The ogival brick construction of 1270 is today's cathedral, a three-naved basilica with chapels surrounding the chancel built in the same way as of *Lübeck*'s St. Mary's Church.

Until 1648, Schwerin remained the see of the (catholic) bishop and of the religious administration of the bishopric. Rivalities between nobility and clergy, their struggles for power and more territory would hamper the development of a city burghership for centuries. Although a city council seems to have existed as early as the thirteenth century, it was always overshadowed by the Mecklenburg regency.

The Cathedral, the city and Castle Island from the west. Hand-coloured drawing, 1605

Between 1330 and 1340, the city got what was essential for medieval cities: a massive city wall of granite blocks, five feet strong. A few relics have been preserved in *Burgstrasse*. The wall stood its test as a bulwark when Albrecht II besieged Schwerin from March to December 1358.

The city proper lay between the castle in the South-West and the cathedral in the North-East. It was surrounded by a palisade of thick stakes and a moat, and was completely deprived of any possibility for expansion. Between 1330 and 1340, Schwerin received what was typical of medieval fortified cities: five-foot thick wall of massive granite. When the city was besieged by Albrecht II from March to December 1358, the bulwark proved its impregnability. Some remainders of the walls have been preserved at *Burgstrasse* street, while the towers and gates have long since disappeared without trace. At the intersection of the *Puschkinstrasse, Friedrichstrasse,* and *Burgstrasse* streets was the *Schelftor* gate; where today's *Schmiede-strasse* joins *Mecklenburgstrasse* – then a ditch between the castle lake and the artificial *Pfaffenteich* pond – was the *Schmiedetor* gate. The intersection of *Schlosstrasse* and *Mecklenburgstrasse* marks the place where the *Mühlentor* [Mill Gate] once stood. From a traffic point-of-view, Schwerin was definitely situated in a bad place: Access from *Wismar* and *Lübeck* was possible only by using the dam at *Mühlentor* gate. The important commercial roads, however, passed by at a distance, so Schwerin was soon commercially overtaken by newer communities such as the Hanseatic cities of *Wismar* and *Rostock*.

Johann Hertzog Magnus Szonn
Hertzog zu Mecklburg Furst zu Wen
den Grauc zu Swerin der Lande Rostock
Vnnd Stargardt Herr

Judittha sein gemahell Graue Ottens
der Hoia tochter. Catharina Hertzog
vonn Sachssenn der Herrn zu Enger
Schwester

Schwerin As Dukal Residence

In 1348, the German Emperor Charles IV. [of Moravia, a descendant of the Luxemburg family] – who resided in Prague – promoted Mecklenburg to the rank of a dukedom, not without reason, for the Sorb princes Albrecht II and Johann had been helpful in the emperor's struggle for *Mark Brandenburg*. After the death of the Counts of Schwerin, Albrecht II bought the county from the heirs, including the castle that became the Duke's residence.

As a residence and through the donations of the clergy (Franciscan monastery, *Heilig-Geist-Haus* [Holy Spirit Hall], and *St. Georgs Hospital*), Schwerin – despite its unfavorable traffic position – became the political and cultural centre of Mecklenburg especially during the Renaissance and Reformation periods.

While Albrecht VII remained true to the old creed, his brother Henry V. made Heinrich Möllens protestant court chaplain and had two of Luther's scholars, Martin Oberländer and Aegidius Faber work here. Under John Albrecht I (1547–76), the Lutheran State Church was established in 1549. Erhart Altdorfer, brother of the famous Regensburg-based painter Albrecht Altdorfer, was named painter to the court of Schwerin and is said to have illustrated the genealogy of the Schwerin house. Bernhard Hederich from *Freiberg* wrote the first chronicle of the City of Schwerin here at the Franciscan monastery, and the geographer Tilemann Stella (1525-89) drew the first map of Mecklenburg.

A prince who wanted to make Schwerin the »Florence of the North« would not let the castle be sober and grey. Just like the Principal Court in *Wismar*, the facade of Schwerin Castle was given sculptural ornaments in red *terracotta*. Though refurbished, they are still to be seen on the Castle's lake front.

At the Historical Museum on *Grosser Moor*, a city model helps you to picture Schwerin in the mid-sixteenth century. City life was concentrated around the Market: City Hall, the City Weighhouse, butchers', fishmongers' and bakers' stands, all kinds of sales stands grouped around the market waure. In the fifteenth century, twelve crafts were registered, among them tanners, butchers, blacksmiths, cloth-makers, wool-weavers, bakers, shoemakers and furriers. Fishing in the watery surroundings as well as brewing played an important role. But after all, the city had scarcely more than 3,000 inhabitants, and only twelve streets or rather lanes!

The low, irregularly standing half-timbered houses with their thatched or shingled roofs were just large enough for one family. The building material of that time – wood and clay bricks – was not very fire-resistant, and in fact, Schwerin's city history, like that of many other medieval cities experienced

Folio page from the Schwerin Manuscript, 1526

Schwerin in the year 1640. Engraving by Merian

several devastating fires, two of them in the sixteenth century (1531 and 1558), and four in the seventeenth (1626, 1651, 1690, 1697). Therefore, today's visitors will look in vain for medieval buildings. Only the cathedral, parts of the Castle and the Cathedral Chapter building of 1574 survived the great fires.

There was further destruction during the Thirty Year's War (1618-48). The famous *Merian* engraving from 1640 shows the extensive bulwarks that the city had erected for its defence. They seem to have been as massive as the bastions of the fortress of *Dömitz* built in 1554-65 that have been preserved to the present. Nevertheless, they could not save the city from sieges. An old tale, though, relates that the castle ghost called *Petermännchen* drove the imperial general Duke Wallenstein out of town, making him take his residence at *Güstrow* castle:

»As soon as the great commander had gone to bed, the ghost would prick and tickle him all night. He would throw over the chairs, then again take the blanket from Wallenstein's bed and whizz around with it. The general – he had always been quite superstitious – feared that a misfortune might strike him and called for his astronomer Seni.« But the next night was even worse: *»In his room a regular snaring noise could be heard. The moon was shining and in the faint light the scared duke saw that the Petermännchen ghost was threatening him with a blinking sword. Wallenstein tried to protect himself using his arm. At the same moment, the great painting of the legitimate duke*

The city's centre in the mid-eighteenth century.

that had been hanging over the bed fell off its nail, burying the general underneath...«

Population numbers show the devastating effects of the Thirty Years' War: Of some 300,000 Mecklenburg inhabitants before the war, only 50,000 were left – just one out of six survived! Many villages were deserted. Unclaimed land was given to the landed gentry, many a surviving farmer was forced into serfdom and bondage. The moral breakdown was also reflected in the increasing number of witch-trials. Many of the trial proceedings have been preserved, the majority dating from the 1660s and showing that the so-called witches were »roasted« on the stake.

Duke Christian I of Mecklenburg-Schwerin who reigned from 1658 to 1692 preferred to stay at the court of Louis XIV. – the Roi Soleil – and took the name of Louis (Ludwig) in his honour. As he died without children, his nephew Friedrich Wilhelm succeeded him and contested the rights to the throne claimed by the son-in-law of Gustav Adolf von Mecklenburg-Güstrow. In 1701, the Hamburg Settlement treaty gave his rival control of *Stargard* and the Dukedom of *Ratzeburg*. From that time the Dukedom of *Mecklenburg-Strelitz* existed besides the Dukedom of Schwerin.

Schwerin During The Eighteenth Century

In 1704, Friedrich Wilhelm decreed the »Principal Mecklenburg Ranking Order«. It started with rank one for the *Secret President of the Council* and ended with rank 24 for coach drivers and timber-men. Mayors and members of the city councils were ranked between 15 and 18, the court painters only at 20. This social classification of the people remained valid in Schwerin beyond the year 1918! The Mecklenburg Low German poet Rudolf Tarnow makes fun of the yearning for rank and title when he writes of one »Mrs. Totally-Secret-Minsterial-Deputy-File-Carrier Besendal«.

One of the duke's wiser decrees, dated 1705, concerned the »Declaration of the Extension of the hitherto so-called *Schelfe* [shelf] near the Old Residence City and Fortress Schwerin«. As a consequence of this decree, the baroque *Neustadt* or *Schelfstadt* was built to a regular design with a rectangular market square and a church of its own (1708–13 by Jacob Reutz). When his sucessor, the imperious and vain Karl Leopold had ruled so viciously as to fall from grace not only with the City of Rostock, but also with the whole nobility, an imperial commission deposed him and called his brother Christian Ludwig to the post of governor in 1728. The regular investiture to the dukedom followed in 1747 after Karl Leopold's death.

The reign of Christian Ludwig II' had positive cultural effects. During his youth, he had travelled throughout Europe and had fallen for the Arts when visiting Rome. But his collections were severely damaged when during a fire in the city of *Grabow* in 1725 *Grabow* castle burnt. He achieved the council's consent that his son Friedrich might travel through the Netherlands, Belgium and France with a visit to England. Besides his diplomatic tasks the latter established contacts to artists and art agents. Thus important works of the Dutch painters collections and of eighteenth century art came to Schwerin.

A new chapter was also opened in the history of the theatre. The famous Schönemann theatre company appeared on stage in 1740, featuring Konrad Ekhof, Conrad Ernst Ackermann, and Charlotte Schröder. From 1751, the »Mecklenburg Court Comedians« were paid wages. In 1753, Ekhof opened the first German theatre academy in Schwerin. His bust near the theatre commemorates this achievement.

The *Schleifmühle* [Grinding Mill] in the castle gardens was used for grinding and smoothing stones and can still be seen in working order today. From the reconstruction of the castle to about 1857, the mill produced tables, mantlepieces, baptistries, epitaph plates and many more items mostly from local granite. Goldsmiths and tin casters played an important role in the trades and crafts. This was also the period of the refurbishment of the *Schlossgarten* gardens by Jean Legeay (1748–65). A channel and waterside shrubs were created, fourteen sculptures from the workshops of the Dresden-based sculptor Balthasar Permoser were erected.

As there had been trouble over the access to power, Christian Ludwig II set up the *Constitutional Agreement* that divided power between the duke and the council. The administration distinguished between the domain, the

Ludwigslust Palace in mid-nineteenth century.

nobility and the cities. The council was to take its seat at *Malchin* and *Sternberg* in turns. Schwerin's importance decreased when in 1756 the new duke, *Friedrich der Fromme* [Frederick the Pious] moved his residence to *Ludwigslust*. His reasons are unknown, and the move was surprising as *Ludwigslust* lacked everything you would expect for a residency. There was but a small hunting castle, a huge park and the tiny village of *Klenow*. Everything else had to be built from scratch. In honour of his father, Duke Frederick called the place »*Ludwigslust*« [Ludwig's Joy], and a new baroque castle was constructed between 1765 and 1770.

But maybe the pious Friedrich was just looking for solitude – after all, times were not good at all. The Prussian king Frederick the Great was enrolling soldiers, the Seven Years' War between Prussia and Austria gobbled up men, money and merchandise. To the Prussian king, Mecklenburg was something like »a big bag of flour. You hit it, and there will be always some more flour to fall out!« The population felt the squeeze, as a drawing by an unknown artist in Schwerin's engravings collection proves. It shows a peasant being addressed by a Prussian rider: »Give what you have!« The peasant turns over his money bag and answers: »Here's my sweat and blood!«. A wife cries out in despair: »If you have taken my husband, take my children, too!« At the same time, David Matthieu painted his series »Glorious images of a meagre time« – nobility in silk and velvet. And Dietrich Findorff engraved the »coppers of the most prominent prospects of *Ludwigslust*«, a castle reflecting the influence of both *Sanssouci* palace, the seat of the Prussian king, and the »No sorrows« ideal of the period.

The architect Johann Joachim Busch who had given *Ludwigslust* the exterior of a residencial town, was given some commissions in Schwerin. He designed the *Marien-Palais* or *Neustädtisches Palais* (1776), the so-called New Building on the Market (1783-85), today part of the History Museum, and the house of the master mason Barca in *Ritterstrasse* Nos. 14-16.

During the non-residential period, the population of Schwerin had tripled, from 3,288 in 1764 to 9,986 in 1819. The bourgeoisie had enhanced their standard of living, the ideals of the French revolution – liberty, equality, fraternity – fell on fertile ground. In 1790, the Schwerin craftsmen revolted against the rise of food prices, letters of complaint were handed in to the Magistrate, and the first strikes were organized. In 1800, the continuing famine led to the so-called »Butter Revolutions«. In 1802, the Schwerin timber-men went on strike, asking for wage increases. The social and political tension of the early nineteenth century culminated in a series of strike and riot actions of pre-proletarian classes, such as in the Schwerin Mint Riot in 1830.

French Occupation And »*Vormärz*« Period

The era of Enlightenment tried to embrace all areas of life with its reforms, and it is under these aspects that Frederick the Pious introduced compulsory education for everyone in 1756. In 1764 a general Song Book for the State Church was decreed, in 1769 torture was abolished and the number of church holidays reduced, but attempts to install a university at *Bützow* did not get very far. When Frederick died without children, his nephew Friedrich Franz I succeeded to the regency, which he held from 1785 to 1815. Although Mecklenburg did its best to keep out of the war between Prussia and France, it suffered a lot under the occupation. This period of troops passing and quarteering known as the *Frenchmen Time* left its mark on Schwerin's history, too. After losing the battle of *Jena* and *Auerstedt* on October 14, 1806, General Blücher's 20,000 troops fled, followed by some 80,000 French soldiers. Under the pretext that Mecklenburg had allowed Russian troops to pass the year before, the country was declared French territory by Napoleon on November 28 and the French general and new governor Laval took Schwerin Castle as his residency. According to the legend, the *Petermännchen* ghost dealt with him as he had treated Wallenstein two centuries before, but Laval is said to have kept the matter hushed up in order not to be laughed at by the people. The French loved the dukal art collection, and the best pieces were shown at the *Louvre* in Paris, albeit for a short period only.

After the peace treaty of *Tilsit*, the French left Mecklenburg and Schwerin. But the duchy still depended on France and had to join the *Rheinbund* [Rhine Association, an association of German states under French rule]. Friedrich Franz I had to mobilize 1,714 troops for Napoleon's campaign against Russia in 1812. After the Russian victory over the French, Friedrich Franz I left the

Paulsstadt area in the mid-nineteenth century.

Rhine Association and on March 25, 1813, he called his people to rise against foreign occupation. A national independence movement emerged similar to the one in Prussia. The most famous troops were *Lutzow's Free Corps* including the patriotic poet Theodor Körner, who died in a battle at Rosenberg near Schwerin on August 26, 1813.

At the Congress of Vienna, both *Mecklenburg-Schwerin* and *Mecklenburg-Strelitz* were elevated to the rank of Grand Dukedoms on June 17, 1815. Since that time, the Mecklenburg ruler was titled Grand Duke, Schwerin became the »Capital of The Grand Dukedom Mecklenburg-Schwerin«. Both Mecklenburg states joined the *Deutscher Bund* [German Federation], an association of the German states that lasted from 1815 to 1866.

During the next few years, the conservative policy of Prince Metternich within the German Federation had its effects on Schwerin, too: Political measures as declared in the *Karlsbad Treaty* of 1819 declared war on any national, democratic, liberal, or revolutionary movements and attmpted to re-establish the old order.

Despite the political oppression in this period of restoration, opposition movements were formed in Schwerin, too.

Following the example of the French July Revolution of 1830, the »*Schweriner Münzaufstand*« [Schwerin Coins Upheaval] broke out in September of the same year.

A currency reform to the disadvantage of the poorest classes made the minor craftsmen and labourers call out for better living conditions. The military fought the riot and shot one Anton Starost, roper, in front of Schwerin Mint building.

Grand Dukal Residence

After Friedrich Franz I had died at the age of 80 after a reign of fifty years, his grandson Paul Friedrich succeeded to the throne in 1837. He moved his residency from *Ludwigslust* back to Schwerin, and this did the city's development a lot of good. Although his rule lasted for five years only, many representative buildings were constructed that completely changed the city's face. The *Paulsstadt* area carrying his name was developed under his reign, and the *Paulsdamm* [Paul's dam] across the lake was made. The area around *Pfaffenteich* lake is based on his ideas.

Paul Friedrich is commemorated by a bronze statue by Christian Daniel Rauch near the castle. Monuments were also erected to his wife Alexandrine: As a daughter of the Prussian king Friedrich Wilhelm III and of Queen Louise she doubtlessly had her share in the attempts to get Schwerin out of its provinciality.

But the architect who gave Schwerin's downtown a design of its own was Georg Adolph Demmler (1804–86). Son of a chimney-sweep, he grew up in *Güstrow* and had an excellent education at the Berlin Academy with Karl Friedrich Schinkel and Johann Gottfried Schadow. In 1823, he entered the Mecklenburg service as assistant court architect, a protegé of the then Heiring Grand Duke Paul. In 1837, he was promoted to senior court architect, in 1841 he became chief architect.

When naming the constructions he designed it becomes obvious that these are the buildings that still determine the city's appearance: the *Kollegiengebäude* at *Schlosstrasse*, the *Marstall* [Court stables], the Arsenal, the facade of City Hall, the Court of Justice on *Schelfstrasse*, the City Hospital at *Werderstrasse*, as well as rows of buildings on the square in front of the railway station and around the *Pfaffenteich* lake. It was he who had the artifical lake encircled in stonework and the swamps at its shores converted to dry land. Demmler himself lived in a palace on the intersection of *Arsenal* and *Mecklenburgstrasse* streets, richly decorated in Florentine palace style – an adequate place for the »*Ministre sans portefeuille*« as he was called due to his great influence.

Demmler's Court Theatre of 1836 has not survived. It was victim of a fire in 1882 – like its predecessor. The palace at the Old Gardens was not completed, its foundations were used in 1877–82 to create today's Museum. Some of Demmler's genial plans for the expansion of the city, too, did not get beyond the planning stage. Nevertheless he was given free reign to

Georg Adolph Demmler, architect to the Court of Schwerin

convert his impressions of Berlin into a broad-minded architectural design for Schwerin.

The following statement gives an impression of how intensely his contemporaries felt the changes that Demmler's buildings brought to the face of the city: *»Since the residence of the Grand Ducal family moved from dull Ludwigslust to Schwerin, a vivid urban life-style has replaced the peaceful, amost rural life and our ways have been overcast with a certain noblesse, although it did not affect the pecularities of the Mecklenburg popular character too much. Many a shack had to give in under the Grand Duke's building projects, their place has been*

The Grand Ducal Castle at Schwerin, engraving by J. Gottheil.

taken by palaces that would easily suit any of Germany's capitals (…). Gallant liveried servants, shiny coaches, well-dressed gentlemen and lavishly ornated ladies, lieutenants in gala dress and the like fill the streets. Parades and court dances, masquerades and the theatre form a constant flow of distractions that have completely overturned the former simple ways of living. Haughtiness has seized the citizens who try to imitate the nobility in every respect (…).«

The refurbishment of the castle was a challenge of its own. The task was to create a representative entity from a muddle of different constructions from various eras and styles. Although the famous architects Stöler, Willebrand and Semper had presented their plans, Demmler was to win. After extensive travels he proposed his third project which was accepted. He was commissioned by Friedrich Franz II who is remembered by the huge horseback sculpture at the Castle Gardens' entrance created by Ludwig Brunow in 1893.

In 1843, the old part of the castle was pulled down. Only the Renaissance parts of the lakeside wing were included in the new design. The exterior aspect was completely changed, as you will easily notice when comparing it with older pictures.

Demmler proved to be a wonderful organizer not only in constructional matters, but also in financial and insurance issues. He proposed social security schemes for accidents and illness by installing benefits for such cases – a wise decision considering that 152 accidents were reported during the four years of reconstruction of the castle.

View from St. Paul's church on old Schwerin, 1865.

Georg Adolph Demmler was also one of Schwerin's leading democrats. In the middle of the construction activities, the 1848 revolution broke out. In a moderate way, the unrest also reached Schwerin. Friedrich Franz II abolished the old constitution of 1755 and decreed a new State Constitution for Mecklenburg-Schwerin on October 10, 1849. This new constitution granted among others a number of civil rights (freedom of press, gathering and associations) as well as the abolishment of physical punishment and peasant serfdom. But already in 1850 the powers of Reaction abolished these liberal laws. Demmler's engagement for civil rights led to his dismissal in 1851. He was succeeded by August Stüler who made several changes to the facade, among them the giant mounted figure of the Obotrite prince Niklot.

On May 26, 1857, the new palace was inaugurated.
»*At the sound of guns, the ringing of bells and all kinds of court splendour. … Church service reception of delegations, presentation of banners to eleven Schwerin crafts that had excelled in the construction, banquet, illumination, torchlight parade and a special performance at the theatre … ›Johann Albrecht‹, an opera by Flotow*«.

Even a medal had been coined for the occasion. Demmler was awarded the medal in gold, but the Order of the Red Eagle from the king's hand he did not receive. With the new palace having a throne hall and the ancestors' gallery, Schwerin went up in rank among the residencial cities. The palace was a symbol for the continuity of the old powers.

Contemporary authors criticized the conservative spirit that reigned in Schwerin. In »*Mecklenburg. Ein Jahrbuch für alle Stände*« [annual manual for all classes] we find: »The railway came too early here, for speed is a thing we fear« and »We're almost scared of industry, it would not suit feudality«.

The first railway line to *Hagenow* opened in 1847, from 1848–50 the line to *Rostock* and *Wismar* was constructed, in 1888 the extension to *Crivitz*, one year later to *Ludwigslust-Dömitz*. In 1890, lines to *Parchim*, *Wittenburg* and *Gadebusch* were added. Minor industries such as iron casting plants, distilleries, steam sawmills, breweries, print shops, cork. lacquer and varnish factories, a brickyard and a piano manufactury attracted workers and brought about social changes. Between 1861 and 1863 the population grew by a thousand, between 1869 and 1871 by 2,000 to a total of some 23,000 inhabitants. All kinds of associations and societies boomed, and the Social Democratic Labour Party founded in 1869 gained increasing influence.

Industrialisation And World War I

In 1874, the *Siegessäule* [Victory Column] at the Old Gardens was erected to commemorate the Franco-Prussian War of 1870/71 in which Mecklenburg troops had participated. It is topped by a statue of *Megalopolis* representing Mecklenburg, cast from captured French guns, and it bears the names of the dead troopers on the base.

The Reparation payments due by France allowed for a boom in construction during the next two decades or so. Public buildings like the Museum (1882) at *Alter Garten*, the new Central Railway Station (1889/90) and the Main Post Office (1892–97) were set up, the Theatre was reconstructed (1883–86). In 1888 through 1892, the spire (by the Court Architect Georg Daniel) that still dominates the city's silhouette was added to the medieval cathedral. Simultaneously, rows of uniform houses with gloomy back yards were built in the suburban and *Paulsstadt* areas.

Traffic planning went at a rather slow pace: »*One in front, one behind, and no one in the middle*«, that's what they said on the streets. And they meant the horse railways that were not accepted by the Schwerin population. The tram fared better when it was introduced in 1881. Tourism increased: while in 1880 some 31,000 non-residents visited the city, their number had grown to 50,000 by 1910.

The city administration had to adapt itself to technical progress, too.

Inauguration of Berwald's fountain »Rescue from The Sea«, 1911

At the turn of the century, the Schwerinians had steamships built in *Kiel* that were to carry such names as »Friedrich Franz«, »Herzogin Alexandrine«, »Niklot« and »Obotrit« and were used for pleasure trips to *Kaninchenwerder* [which in English means »Rabbit bank« or »Rabbit Island«] and to *Zippendorf*. In 1913, the Fokker company moved their airplane factory from Berlin to Schwerin, and an aviation school and an airfield were set up at *Görries*.

In the early twentieth century, the builders' taste was dominated by the *Art-Déco*-Style. As far as the city centre was concerned, nothing more than closing the gaps in the rows of houses was possible. Examples of the style can be found in the *Landeshauptarchiv* [Main State Archive] on *Graf-Schack-Allee* (by P. Ehmig 1909–11), in the former »*Stadthallen*« Halls on *Marienplatz* square (1909), the department store at *Mecklenburgerstrasse* 19–23 (by H. Stoeffers in 1910), and the former Mecklenburg Savings Bank on *Arsenal* and *Wismarsche Strasse* streets by *G. Roensch* in 1909. The living quarters near the bus station were built on swampy ground and seem to be doomed regardless of their beautiful facades. For the *Art-Déco*-sculpture we should mention Hugo Berwald's »Rescue from The Sea«, a fountain dated from 1911, today situated in front of the Central Railway Station.

In 1914, World War I broke out. The city chronicler Wilhelm Jesse writes that the news of »General Mobilization and War« was received with national enthusiasm: *»It can be easily explained that such an attitude had to prevail in Schwerin and among a population whose train-of-thought is so clearly determined by the court, the state officers and the army (…). The joy over the successful campaigns of the local regiments – who had won their first honours at Lièges – and the great expectations sustained by the official reports were not notably diminished by the grief for the dead and wounded, long lists of which would soon reach home.«*

The civilian population was increasingly asked to make sacrifices. *»The War affected all areas of life much deeper than any of the wars and sufferings of the past (…). Like a heavy load, gaining in weight every month, the War affected every single person.«* Food was rationed, trades, crafts and traffic came to a halt. Development plans for the *Totendamm* and *Domhof* areas were set aside, but the Court of Justice was finished in 1916 and the airfield at *Görries* was enlarged. The Fokker plants employed hundreds of workers. Near *Holthusen* a great ammunition factory was built after 1916, other existing industries were integrated into the war production process. Tourism and entertainment practically disappeared. *»Only various events for patriotic and charity purposes, Flowers' Days, War exhibitions, Bazaars, nailing actions on the cathedral doors were abundant, and the collection of money and material for the most varied goals, like Books, Metal and Wool Weeks appealed to the population's goodwill for voluntary contributions.«*

People had enough of the War, and hunger accelerated the change of mood: In July 1917 demonstrations broke out, and in January 1918 the 1,000 workers at the Fokker plants went on strike. »Down with war!« was the parole. On November 6, 1918, the troops joined the demonstrators. Officers were disarmed, the railway station, the post and telegraph offices as well as the police stations were seized by the labourers. A Labour and Soldiers' Council was installed and the government was asked to dissolve. On November 14, 1918, the Grand Duke abdicated from his throne after emperor Wilhelm II had abdicated in Berlin on November 9. A bourgeois coalition government was installed.

The War was lost. The Treaty of Versailles stipulated reparations and loss of territories. In 1919, the new National Council met for the first time at *Weimar*. After the first elections, a general Constitution was installed for the whole of Germany. But the new state, the *Weimar Republic*, would not remain uncontested. During the so-called *Kapp-Putsch* that was to re-establish the old [i.e. feudal] order, riots started in Schwerin, too. On March 15, 1920, there was heavy fighting between the Arsenal and the Central Post Office during which the troops commanded by General Lettow-Vorbeck killed 13 male and two female workers. The Central Post Office bears a commemorative plate to the victims of this struggle against the right-wing putschists.

Marienplatz square around 1930.

The economic situation did not change for the better, either. Money became scarce, above all small change, as the coins had been melted into shells. The management of Fokker could not pay the wages and asked the Ministry of Finance for permission to issue scrip money. After quite a while and heated discussions the permit was granted.

As other cities had filed for the same permit, the Tourist Board of *Rostock* intervened: The so-called *Reuter-Money* designed by artists was issued for some 70 towns and villages of Mecklenburg. Today, this scrip money [or rather these bonds issued by the various city administrations to be changed into »real« currency by a certain date] has become an interesting collectors' item.

The global economic crisis and the inflation cast their shadows over Schwerin. Greater development plans were inconcievable. The available funds were just sufficient for building a few industrial premises at *Görries*, an industrial port on *Ziegelsee* lake and a small residential area along *Werderstrasse*. One exception was the *Niklot*-School on *Obotritenring*, built in 1929 and opened the next year. At the end of 1932, 4,707 inhabitants out of 53,621 were unemployed.

The NS Era And World War II

The rise to power of the NSDAP [the Nazi party] brought noticeable changes to Schwerin, too. The city became State and District Capital under the *Gauleiter* Friedrich Hildebrandt. It seemed to prosper, constructions were under way: Barracks on *Ludwigsluster Chaussee* and on *Güstrower Strasse* roads, red brick houses in the suburbs, at *Neumühle*, on *Güstrower Strasse* and – for the local Nazi prominence – at *Tannhof*. The airfield at *Görries* – de-militarized after World War I – served the *Luftwaffe*. In 1936, the population of Schwerin doubled through the integration of surrounding villages such as *Medewege, Wickendorf, Warnitz, Krebsförden, Muess, Kaninchenwerder* and *Ziegelwerder*.

Like everywhere in Germany, the *Führer*'s followers dominated not only public life, they also kept a watchful eye on everyone who could be suspected of »non-German« behaviour or ideas. The suspects were above all intellectuals, authors and artists and anyone likely to have opposing ideas, such as communists and socialists. »Enemies of the people« would disappear over night. The Concentration Camp nearest to Schwerin was *Reiherhorst* near *Wöbbelin*. There were prisons as well to keep custody of political prisoners. In 1934, 22 citizens of Schwerin were convicted of treason and sentenced to long prison terms. The persecution of Jews culminated in the so-called »*Reichskristallnacht*« that also saw the destruction of the synagogue on *Schlachtermarkt*. The deportation and persecution of Jewish people is documented in a Jewish memorial erected in 1951 in the court at *Schlachterstrasse* No.3. Resistance to the brutal, totalitarian system came mostly from social democrats and communists. Among their many activities was the distribution of flyers, help and assistance to endangered persons and the organization of common resistance with the POWs and foreign detainees. The nucleus of this resistance was the STALAG II E camp on today's *Grosser Dreesch*.

World War II inflicted heavy wounds on Schwerin. In 1940 and during the last weeks of the war, bombs hit streets near the *Schlachthof*, near the tram depot and above all *Görries* airfield. The old city, however, remained more or less untouched. Schwerin suffered 4,200 dead. Towards the end of the war the city was full of refugees. They raised the number of inhabitants from 64,000 to 94,000. But the Nazi would not yet give in. Even on May 2, 1945, the day of liberation, the SS publicly hanged the teacher Marianne Grunthal who had expressed her satisfaction over Hitler's death. And a second event documents the extent of dramatic developments: The same day, a group of starving prisoners from concentration camps reached the city at *Raben Steinfeld*, after ten days of marching from *Sachsenhausen* and *Ravensbrück*. Over 6,000 out of 33,000 had died during this march. Hence this tragic event is referred to as »The March of Death«. In commemoration, a series of rocks with inscriptions mark the march route, and in 1976 the sculptor Gerhard Thieme designed a memorial with a statue of a crying mother.

On the same day, Anglo-American troops reached the city from the west, while the Soviet Army reached the east banks of Lake Schwerin. In accordance with the agreement of Yalta the line of demarcation was laid out so as to add Schwerin and the western part of Mecklenburg to the Soviet Zone. On July 1, the Soviet *Kommandantura* was installed in Schwerin. The city had surrendered without a fight.

A New Start

The reconstruction of economic and cultural life was not easy: In the first month after the end of the war, there were 557 deaths compared to only 162 births. Diphtheria and typhus broke out. The number of serious cases was estimated at 8,000. Due to the closure of the border with the Western sectors, the whole region had been reduced to a neglected border area. Schwerin was cut off from its former trading partners Hamburg and *Lübeck*. Enormous reparations demands by the Soviet Union and the dismantling of industrial plants caused additional damage to the battered economy.

On April 7, 1946, the social democrats and the communists of Mecklenburg united to form the new SED [*Sozialistische Einheitspartei Deutschlands* – Socialist United Party of Germany] at the *Capitol* Cinema and used the motto »The union of labour parties means the abolishment of the nobility, reactionaries and militarists«. Once again, people disappeared overnight, and complete silence was kept about camps like the one in *Fünfeichen* near *Neubrandenburg*. Many of those who had been expropriated through the land reforms or who were considered »capitalists« because they owned major industries, or those who had played a major role in the NS party or government or army had fled in time to areas controlled by the western allies. This movement gradually spread to all groups of the population, especially the younger who left if they could. It increased when the psychological pressure grew, when so-called »campaigns« were under way to enforce government decisions like the collectivization of agriculture, the reduction of private trade and craft enterprises or the de-privatization of apartment blocks.

On October 7, 1949, the German Democratic Republic was founded. On December 2, thousands of Schwerin citizens gathered at the Central Station to listen to the G.D.R.'s first president, *Wilhelm Pieck*. The former federal states were broken up into smaller units by the administration reform in 1952, and Schwerin became district capital which led to the foundation of many state, political and scientific institutions over the following years.

Construction activities started with the declared intention to raise the city out of the traditional backwardness of agricultural Mecklenburg and to develop it into a »modern socialist centre« based on industry. The *Klement-Gottwald-Works* which produced naval supplies from cranes to hydraulic rudders were enlarged as were other industrial sectors such as textile and timber industries.

Demolition work at Großer Moor.

In the 1950s, new city quarters such as the *Weststadt* and *Lankow* were developed, in 1956 the first skyscraper on *Lamprechtsgrund* and in the years 1959-62 the Sports and Congress Hall for 8,200 people were built. In 1956, a zoo was founded, in 1962 an observatory with a planetarium. Two years later the new landmark of Schwerin, the TV Tower at *Zippendorf* rose to its full height of over 400 feet housing even a coffee shop. In the late 60s and early 70s, schools, supermarkets, nursery schools and hospitals were added to the new city quarters. The *Weststadt* area now had some 14,000 inhabitants, *Lankow* some 17,000. After the south of Schwerin had been declared an industrial focus in 1971 with plastic industry, leather, hydraulics and concrete prefab-works, housing development was expanded.

With 60,000 inhabitants, the *Grosser Dreesch* quarter developed into Schwerin's largest suburb. Even today almost 50% of the population live here. Although this quarter is equipped with schools, supermarkets, restaurants, coffee-shops, libraries and services, it is still an appendix. The five-storeyed apartment blocks from prefabricated concrete slabs lack a true atmosphere despite the lake and shores nearby. The »real« Schwerin is still the old city. But in the old city houses began to crumble. Whole blocks have disappeared or are no longer recognizable, even if the new buildings tried to imitate their predecessors in size and shape. This is true of the oldest parts around *Tappenhagen*, *Salzstrasse*, and *Glaisinstrasse* streets. Also the *Grosser Moor* connecting *Werderstrasse* and *Puschkinstrasse* has completely changed. Despite some destruction, the area around the Market and *Schlachtermarkt*

34

At Großer Dreesch.

has managed to preserve its old-fashioned atmosphere. But the architectural substance of the *Schelfstadt* is endangered, and citizens' movements have been calling for the preservation of this quarter. Some old single buildings like the *Wöhlersche Weinstuben* [Woehler's Wine House] seem to be doomed.

The locals as much as the tourists enjoy the pedestrian zones installed in the 70s at the *Mecklenburg*, *Schmiede*, *Puschkin*, and *Schlosstrasse* business quarters. Although some of the decisions and mistakes of the past did harm the exterior of the city, Schwerin can still boast to be a place with a special atmosphere. »One of the most beautiful squares of Germany with its circle of beautiful buildings and its unique view on the blue surface of the Big Lake« is what Edmund Schroeder calls the Old Garden. Once but a swamp, then the glacis of the fortress, later gardens and military exercising grounds, it is today's meeting place for the Schwerin inhabitants, and this was where the great demonstrations in the autumn of 1989 took place.

Autumn 1989: Times Are Changing

The first public meeting took place on October 23, 1989. The *Neues Forum* movement had properly informed the police and had been issued a permit for the mass gathering. Shortly before the event started, this permit was revoked, but it was too late to cancel the meeting. So the District Leaders of the S.E.D. party decided to seize the opportunity and to use the mass meeting for their own purposes. Anonymous leaflets appeared, calling for participation. Everyone believed – as they should have – that the *Neues Forum* had made this effort. The S.E.D. chartered buses to take workers from industrial plants at *Wittenberge, Boizenburg, Gadebusch* and elsewhere to Schwerin. The *Neues Forum* noticed this just in time to call their supporters to the Cathedral at an earlier hour. After a service there, they marched through the centre with lit candles in their hands until they finally reached the Old Garden. There the two groups stood face to face: the *Neues Forum* on the Theatre side, the Party supporters around the *Siegessäule* [Victory Column].

When people noticed they had been had, they started changing sides. There were heated discussions with the representatives of the Party. The chairman fled through the back door to the *Kollegiengebäude* building nearby that served as the Party Seat. Regional papers printed protest letters concerning this affair. From then, Monday – just as in *Leipzig* – became Schwerin's demonstration day. Only much later the public were informed that the *Stasi* [State Security Intelligence Service] and armed groups had been hidden in ambush, ready to interfere with machine-guns at any given time. But here, too, the revolution passed quite peacefully. The number of demonstrators increased every time – finally it was estimated at 100,000 (out of 130,000 inhabitants). People came from the surrounding villages, the railings around *Pfaffenteich* were decorated with candles as well as the window sills of the Arsenal (the Police Headquarters) and of the Court of Justice Building on Demmler Square (which was the *Stasi* Headquarters). After the opening of the borders on November 9, there was great joy. Endless lines of cars moved – or rather did *not* move– on the roads to Lübeck and Hamburg, more stop than go at an average speed of less than three miles an hour. It took sixteen hours to get to Lübeck.

The spiritual and intellectual basis of the »*Wende*« – not a great term, by the way, as this was much more than merely the political *turn of the tide* the word suggests, it was the consequence of a complete social change – was to a great extent due to artists and intellectuals. This is true for the performances at Mecklenburg State Theatre under Christoph Schroth who had gained international acknowledgement for his programme. Among his most succesful productions are his version of »*Faust*« and his »*Entdeckungen*« [Discoveries], a series of well-set events with pieces from antique to modern presented simultaneously on all the available stages.

In late autumn 1989, the premiere of an evening with old folk songs set the audience roaring with joy and triggered real fraternization scenes, for the public had found an elementary feeling of solidarity in the old melodies that had seemed to be lost for so many years. When the authorities tried to prohibit further performances of the piece, the ensemble spoke out in public protest, writing resolutions that were exhibited at the theatre's foyer. Also exhibitions and panel discussions by artistis, meetings of scientists from various disciplines, conferences of authors and publishers served as a forum for the critical

Schwerin 1989 – Candles became the symbol of the political change.

assessment of the recent past. One of the issues, for instance, was the politically dominated and thus very selective and restrictive access to national and regional heritage – from the history of persons to the preservation of monuments. As a result, the demand for change became ever stronger. And many artists and »cultural activists« became both seismographs and actors in the process of social revolution in late 1989, without ever imagining where this process would lead with all its social implications.

The speed was really breathtaking. Elections, elections and elections all over again. Political union. Monetary union. Low-flying helicopters protecting the transfer of money. And then – disenchantment. Unemployment, disconcertment. Competing with *Rostock*, Schwerin was named capital of the newly founded Federal State of *Mecklenburg-Vorpommern*. Today, the castle is the seat of the *Landtag* [State Council], the *Kollegiengebäude* is the residence of the State Government, the Arsenal is the Ministry of Interior, the *Marstall* serves the Ministries of Culture and of Social Matters and Health … The signs are being changed, wherever you look, even streets are being renamed. Schwerin dispalys its new face: Giant bill-boards in place of political *paroles*, shops are being privatized and are changing their design. New colours, new scaffolds, pneumatic drills…

The demands imposed by the aspect of openness towards the world are in conflict with provincial trains-of-thought. Nevertheless, Schwerin should preserve at least a glimpse of dreaminess in its alleys, its parks, its water-birds. And the swans shall continue to have the right-of-way over speeding cars. But alas, hotels, car parks and supermarkets are what the city needs. So let's hope that they will integrate unpretentiously into the existing cityscape without dominating the traditional structures that otherwise would be gone forever!

Cultural Life

Art Collections

Like many famous museums the *Schwerin Art Museum* also started as the ducal »Chamber of Arts and Wonders«. Especially Christian Ludwig II had a well developed sense for the Arts. His interest was mainly devoted to the Dutch paintings of the seventeenth century and to his French contemporary painters. When in 1725 a fire destroyed the major part of his collections at *Grabow* castle he sent his son Frederick on a tour through Europe (1737–39) and had him buy what he could get in the ateliers, at art agents' and at auctions. It is astonishing how many first class drawings, paintings, engravings and sculptures were bought on this tour, especially when considering the limited finances. As early as 1792, a printed catalogue of the paintings at Schwerin Castle was published, containing 695 items. 209 of these paintings were taken to Paris in 1809 by the French, but they came back nine years later – many of them with new frames.

In 1818, paintings, drawings, engravings and craft masterpieces from the heritage of Prince Maximilian of Cologne were added to the collections. In his 1821 catalogue, the court painter and arts administrator Friedrich Christoph Georg Lenthe expressed the wish for one spacious area to present all the works together. But a full-sized museum building could not be considered during the next few years. The collection remained distributed among the castles at Schwerin, *Ludwigslust*, *Neustadt* and *Rostock*.

When Schwerin Castle was refurbished it became necessary to relocate the art collection. The works were put into two adjacent houses in the *Paulsstadt* quarter (on *Alexandrinen* and *Wilhelmstrasse*) and were shown to the public three days a week. At last, in 1862, the Cabinet Councillor Eduard Posch managed to convince the Grand Duke of the necessity »to build a Museum on the very spot where a palace had been planned at the Old Gardens«.

But for the time being the refurbishment of the Castle had absolute priority. Only in late 1877 did the money from French war reparation payments allow for the construction of a Gallery of Arts on the foundations of the Old Gardens palace. The museum was designed in late classicist style by Hermann Willebrand, a scholar of Demmler. The opening took place on October 22, 1882. The first managing director of the museum was Friedrich Schlie, a connoisseur and very able manager. He not only designed the gable frieze representing the marriage of Amor and Psyche, he also ensured a scientific approach to the collections. His »Descriptive catalogue of the works of Old Masters in the Grand Ducal Painting Gallery at Schwerin« was to become a model for scientific catalogue design in the Arts. Between 1896 and 1902, Schlie published the »Inventory of the Art and History Monuments of Mecklenburg«, a basic reference work to the present day.

The Galeriegebäude exhibition building at the Old Garden.

The Museum was enlarged in 1901 and 1912 respectively, and was nationalized six years later. An auction of graphics and prints in 1926 brought enough money to allow for the purchase of contemporary works of national and international importance, e.g. by Max Liebermann and Lovis Corinth. During Word War II most of the collection was kept in safe deposits, in 1961 the objects were transferred back to their original location at the Museum.

Nowadays, the Gallery building at the Old Gardens houses only the Fine Arts. The Mecklenburg Ethnological Collection has been moved to *Schwerin-Muess*, the Pre- and Early History Collection to the Castle. Although some parts of the arts collection are on show at *Güstrow, Ludwigslust* and Schwerin Castles, the space available is far from sufficient to clear the deposits. At present, the collections comprise some 3600 paintings, 52,000 engravings and etchings, 8,000 drawings, 32,000 coins, and some 10,000 items from the applied arts, such as porcelain, fayences, antiques, arms and furniture.

On the upper floor, a collection of Old Masters from the sixteenth to the eighteenth century awaits the visitor. The Dutch and Flemish painters of the seventeenth century make up the majority of works on show. With some 550 paintings, the Schwerin collection from this Golden Age of Dutch painting is the most complete and comprehensive in Germany. Besides the paintings, Schwerin has some 4,000 Dutch engravings from the same period, among

»Peasant company« by A. Brouwer, Staatliches Museum Schwerin.

them 173 by Rembrandt, and the complete graphic works of Adriaen van Ostade, master of rural painting. With some 600 works, eighteenth century painting is well represented, too. Among the most valuable items we find the artistic heritage of the French painter and engraver Jean-Baptiste Oudry. King Louis XV of France's court painter produced excellent animal and hunting scenes, still lives, elegant portraits and a number of landscapes.

On the ground floor of the museum we find above all contemporary art of the twentieth century, but space restrictions allow only for the exhibition of selected examples. The so-called »Church Hall« presents medieval sculptures, altars and minor art objects of mostly Mecklenburg origin. Schwerin's collection of Meissen porcelain is second only to Dresden's. The many objects from the glass and porcelain collection give an impression of the variety of production and of the excellent craftsmanship of the traditional manufacturers and factories. The engravings cabinet with its rich collection of drawings and graphics from the sixteenth to the twentieth century, though, is accessible only upon prior agreement.

As soon as the refurbishment of *Ludwigslust* palace is finished, the collection of court arts of the seventeenth century will be transferred there and shown in the same way as Schwerin Castle displays mostly nineteenth century art. Here on the first intermediate floor a unique gallery of Mecklenburg painting was installed, showing eighteenth to twentieth century works. The exhibits show the way Mecklenburg artists saw nature and art tradition of their home country.

The treasures of Schwerin Museum are larger and of greater importance than visitors are normally aware of. Single pieces and whole collections have been on show abroad, in the Netherlands, France, Poland, Hungary, the former Soviet Union and as far away as Japan, Mexico and Texas.

Ingrid Möller

The Theatre

The tradition of the theatre in Schwerin dates back to the sixteenth century. The chronicles of these years tell us of spiritual plays »in the church« and they relate that scholars and schoolmasters played »*comediae*« in the mid-sixteenth century, receiving a fee from the Duke's purse. Whether the theatre fared well or not depended largely on the ducal court. It was the likes and dislikes of the respective Highnesses which determined whether theatres opened or closed, whether theatre companies were hired or fired. The seventeenth century saw »English comedians« as commercial groups in town, one Mr. Andreas Pandssen as Principal Comedian at court and the first idea of a Court Theatre at the Castle.

The old Theatre.

In 1702, a »Comedy and Green House« is opened on Castle Island by Duke Friedrich Wilhem. After his death in 1713, however, the theatre company falls apart and the house starts to decay. The year 1740, however, marks a change and the beginning of Schwerin's theatre tradition. Duke Christian Ludwig hires the famous Schönemann Theatre Company as »Mecklenburg-Schwerin Court Comedians«. The castle's dancing hall is transformed into a stage, and although the theatre season lasts but one year, in 1750 Johann Friedrich Schönemann comes back to Schwerin to soon become the managing director of the Ducal Theatre. One of his actors is one Konrad Ekhof who will become what the historians of the theatre call the »Father of German Stage Art«. Although trained with the French style, he demands and represents a »naturalist«, i.e. realistic style of acting. In 1753, he becomes the founder of the first German theatre academy at Schwerin. With the death of the art-loving Duke Christian Ludwig II, however, this first heyday of Schwerin theatre comes to a halt. His successor Frederick – nicknamed the Pious – bans all kinds of acting and stage from the city.

Cultural life is revived after Frederick's death. In 1788, the former riding hall and ballroom-house at the Old Garden is transformed into a »real« theatre, serving its purpose until 1831 when it burns down. Georg Adolph Demmler whose buildings still determine the look of the city is commissioned with rebuilding the theatre. In 1836, the new Grand Ducal Court Theatre at the Old Garden is finally completed – with 600 seats a truly representative theatre building. A new era of Schwerin's theatre life starts. For seven years, the composer Friedrich von Flotow manages the theatre and he calls the conductor Georg Alois Schmidt to his side in 1856. Under his leadership, Schwerin becomes the second »Wagnerian« city after Bayreuth and he shapes the court musicians group (in existence since 1563) into one of the leading orchestras of the whole country. Felix Mendelssohn-Bartholdy, Clara Schumann, Joseph Joachim, Camille Saint-Saens as well as Johannes Brahms conduct or perform with the orchestra. Wagner's operas dominate the programme and in 1878, enthusiasts arrive on special trains from Berlin and Hamburg to watch the first performance of the *Valkyrie* outside of *Bayreuth*.

This cultural development is interrupted by a catastrophe: In 1882, Demmler's theatre suffers the fate of its predecessor. During a performance of »Robert and Bertram« the stage is set on fire and the theatre burns down to the ground. It is a gigantic fire that can be seen as far as *Wismar*, *Hugenow* and *Malchin*, if we may trust old documents. Fortunately, there is no panic, the Grand Duke stays in his booth and the orchestra continues playing so that the theatre can be evacuated witn calm. Only one fire-fighter dies in the flames.

But the fire has done a thorough job: Refurbishment is impossible, thus a new building is erected. In 1883, construction begins with difficulties, for the swampy underground calls for solid foundations on pillars. Meanwhile, though, acting goes on: a half-timbered construction on the square in front of the railway station serves as a preliminary theatre, although the performances are said to have suffered from the level of noise along the railway. On October 3, 1886, the neo-baroque Court Theatre built by the architects Daniel, Raspe, and Hartmann is solemnly opened – a place with every possible technical piece of equipment of its time. It is the first building in the city to have electric lighting – long before this commodity finds its way into the citizens' houses –, it offers seating for an audience of a thousand plus a concert hall for 500 people. And one more peculiarity: The total cost is said to have been *lower* than the estimate – quite unique, not only in those days!

At Schwerin Castle Festival.

Schwerin's theatre has remained unchanged on the whole to the present. In the 1940s, the concert hall was transformed into a second, smaller stage hall. One of the »sins« of the cultural policy of the 1950s, a modernization of the interior, is gradually being replaced by a reconstruction of the original. So the Foyer, the entrance hall and the vestibule of the central lounge as well as the »Flotow-Room« present themselves in the splendour of 1886, while the audience sits in a re-designed hall.

The abdication of the Grand Dukes in 1918 completed the history of the Court Theatre – it was renamed »County Theatre« and – in 1926 – »Mecklenburg State Theatre«. And besides serving as a theatre it also housed the State council until 1933. Like most of the old parts of Schwerin, the theatre survived the War without further damage. In 1946, Lucie Höflich founded one of the first post-war theatre schools here.

The post-war theatre history is determined by the work of one person, the managing director Christoph Schroth. He made Schwerin a Mecca for theatre enthusiasts from near and far. He called his concept »Intervening Theatre« and searched for contact with the audience by using the means of the traditional popular theatre in dealing with the issues of the present. The evenings designed by Schroth and his dramaturgist Bärbel Jaksch were called »Discoveries« and involved activities in all rooms and halls, communication, gastronomy, music and performances, with three programmes per night. In early 1990, Schroth went to Berlin, leaving Schwerin to find a new concept. Numerous young actors were engaged who should contribute to give Schwerin a new cultural impulse. Through the cooperation with the neighbouring cities of *Lübeck, Ratzeburg, Kiel* and Hamburg, new perspectives in the development of the theatre were introduced.

Every year, the State Theatre offers 20 to 25 new productions in the sectors of theatre, opera, operetta, musical, ballet and puppeteering. The *Fritz-Reuter-Bühne*, with its Low German programme, too, has become a trade-mark of Schwerin's culture in its sixty years of existence. Since 1993, the months of June und July are used for open-air performances in the Renaissance settings of the Castle's inner court, presenting music theatre and plays. Besides this, since 1994 a European Theatre Festival brings guest performances to various stages and sites at Schwerin.

Music

The classical music scene relies mostly on the traditional *Mecklenburgische Staatskapelle* [State Orchestra] dating back as far as 1563. Besides being the opera orchestra of the State Theatre, the orchestra performs some twenty symphonic concerts at the Theatre every season. The chamber orchestra gives twelve public performances at Schwerin Castle's Throne Hall and at the State Museum per year. There are other chamber music formations of rank, such as a winds quintet, a string quartet and a brass ensemble. According to tradition, Beethoven's Symphony No. 9 is performed every New Year's Eve, featuring the State Orchestra, soloists and chorus of the State Theatre as well as the *Schweriner Singakademie*, a renowned amateur choir.

The second great orchestra was the *Schweriner Philharmonie*. Founded in 1946 as the *Mecklenburgisches Landesorchester*, it should above all »transmit new psychical powers to the choirs, the working communities and the labouring people«. In 1972, the orchestra was renamed *Staatliches Symphonieorchester* [State Symphony Orchestra], performing mainly at the so-called Festive Hall of Schwerin Castle. In 1980, the orchestra was given its final name: *Schweriner Philharmonie*. It played at various venues in the city, even at the *Capitol* Theatre. Due to financial problems the orchestra played its final concert in 1992.

Aerial view of Schwerin Castle.

A survey of the musical life of Schwerin would be incomplete without mentioning sacred music. The main places of performance are the Cathedral, St. Paul's Church and the Castle Church. The highlights of sacred music performances are J. S. Bach's Christmas Oratorio and his Passions as well as the organ concerts at the Cathedral every Wednesday in summer.

Ingrid Möller, Helmut Schultz

Church Life In Schwerin

Christian religion in Mecklenburg dates back to the mid-twelfth century: A Cistercian monk named Berno from *Amelungsborn* abbey in Westphalia came to this region, baptizing, preaching and spreading out Christian creed despite several drawbacks. In 1166 this monk is consecrated as a bishop, five years later he moves his see to Schwerin. Up to the present the Protestant bishop has had his see here, while the Catholics belong to the Hamburg archdiocese since 1995. As

Schwerin was the residency of the Mecklenburg Dukes from the thirteenth century, the clergy and nobility left their mark on the socio-cultural life of the city over the centuries.

Today, Schwerin has seven Protestant and three Catholic communities. The Cathedral, Castle, St. Nicolai (popularly called *Schelf*), St. Pauls', Berno's, Reconciliation (at Lankow) and St. Peters's communities are Lutheran, St. Anna's, St. Martin's, and St. Andrew's parishes are Catholic. Historical developments after the Reformation made the number of Protestants exceed the Catholics by quite a margin, which is reflected in the number and distribution of parishes.

Besides the services as the core of community work, there are numerous religious groups and circles like the Young Communities, Women's and Old Age groups, ecological and peace groups, Bible and conversation rounds. The numerous musical activities of the church communities have already been mentioned. Besides a slow re-introduction of religious education at school, the Lutheran Protestants have preserved the so-called »Christian Education« [i.e. Sunday School] tradition. Children are introduced to biblical history in a suitable way and learn about community life. In 1994, a total of 438 children participated in this (1989: 643; 1990: 593, 1991: 635). Furthermore, the Protestant communities performed 57 baptisms in 1994, 14 weddings and 231 funeral services. In the years before German reunion, the churches' possibilities were limited, above all their P.R. work was hampered. Nevertheless, the communities remained active, and many people found a place for relaxation and encouragement, especially in the regular Peace Prayers. And it was one of these Peace Prayers that started the first great demonstration on October 23, 1989, that was to become so important in Schwerin's history. »Christians do pray first before they go out on the streets« – that was the word. The Cathedral was overcrowded. More than 40,000 people are estimated to have participated in the subsequent demonstration. Participation in the Peace Prayers increased to such an extent over the next few weeks that the services hat to take place in three churches simultaneously.

Yet, with some 13% of Sshwerin's population, Christians remain a minority. As before, many people are loosening their ties with the traditional church, bringing along, among others, great financial problems for the communities. Maintenance of the buildings is very expensive, and the structure of the parishes must be reconsidered. The permanent confrontation with the atheistic communist state had always been a continuous challenge and incentive, but today the Church has to cope with the fact that Christian values and ways of living have lost their attractiveness in today's society and that many people are interested only in material matters.

The matter is different in the social activites of the *Diakonie* and *Caritas* organisations. Numerous *kindergardens* and social centres run by the parishes have become an important factor in the city's life. Information centres for drugs, family, debts etc. are well accepted, and the Catholic church even started running a school. The traditional Lutheran hospital *St. Anna's* had to be closed, other institutions, such as the *Augustenstift* Old Age and Nursing Home were modernized and enlarged. Schwerin houses numerous administrative and other institutions of the two religious communities, such as a theological-educational institute and a preachers' seminary.

Although the parishes and communities will have to cope with less personnel and with limited finances, the churches' presence will continue. Schwerin is unimaginable withouth church life. Services, education, sacred music, social activities – these are the areas where church life is active and always present.

Ludwig Seyfarth

City Tours And Sightseeing

The City's Structure

Schwerin's design has been greatly influenced by given topographical facts, and the lakes indenting the cityscape are the most obvious characteristics. Without any direct link to the city, the castle stands out on an island in the lake. The Old City that extends like an island between the *Burgsee* [Castle Lake], the outskirts of *Lake Schwerin* and *Pfaffenteich* lake is bordered by an irregular pentagon that is walled off by *Mecklenburg, Kloster, Burg,* and *Friedrichstrasse* streets. The street plan is grid-shaped, but due to the geographical situation the streets do not intersect at right angles. The Market lies at the centre of this pentagon, with the Cathedral slightly to the north.

The independent quarter of the *Schelfstadt* built in the early eighteenth century sticks out clearly with its larger territory. While in its southern part the three older radial streets are visible, the northern part is distinguished by its regular rectangular blocks. The square in front of *Schelfkirche* church and the oblong Schelfmarkt square north of it mark the centre of this area. From 1840, the city quickly extended past its medieval borders, first by incorporating the *Pfaffenteich* area in the north-west, then to the west and in the second half of the nineteenth century into the areas between the lakes close to the city. Their beautiful landscape has been used for the construction of campus-like living districts since the early twentieth century. In the 1920s and during the Third Reich new districts were built at *Weststadt* and *Neumühle*.

After World War II – which had left the city practically untouched – the first development activities started in 1955 with the Weststadt construction programme. Here in September 1963, the first »skyscraper« of Schwerin was inaugurated. *Lankow* followed in 1962, and in 1971 the *Grosser Dreesch* quarter was built, both of them suburbs without any closer relation to the historical centre. *Grosser Dreesch* offers housing for some 60,000 people. All houses were prefabricated and built on site.

Market Square

The very centre of Schwerin's Old City is the Market Square. Its rectangular shape dates back to the great fire of 1651, an extension to the north was made in 1783 when the New Building (*Neues Gebäude*) was built. Nevertheless,

Previous pages: View of the city centre with the Cathedral and Pfaffenteich lake; in the background the Schelfstadt area and Lake Schwerin

The Market seen from the Cathedral's spire.

its size is small compared to the market squares of the Hanseatic Cities on the coast, indicating the relatively small economic importance of Schwerin in the past.

Besides the nearby Cathedral, the so-called **Neues Gebäude** [New Building] on the northern face of the square dominates the Market's view. The widespread construction from the early classicist period was built as Market Hall in 1783–85, the wheel and the staff on the gable still commemorate this fact. The traders' building designed by Johan Joachim Busch housed long arched rows of minor shops on its ground floor, and replaced the so-called »Scharren« trade stands that had been used since the Middle Ages. In 1975, the city archives opened an exhibition on the city's history at the New Building and since 1990, the house and the exhibition are part of the Historical Museum that offers its visitors a »Marketplace of History« with permanent and special exhibitions.

On the eastern side of the square we find the **City Hall**, documented in 1351, destroyed several times by fires and always rebuilt on the same site. Only an ogival arcade on the rear facade and the brickwork above it (today the archway of the City Hall Passage) is left of the medieval building. The two half-timbered gables date back to the renovation of 1654, the Tudor style Market facade was built in 134/35 by. G.A. Demmler. The **Golden Rider** on the middle merlon represents the city's coat-of-arms – identical to Henry

City Hall with the Golden Rider.

the Lion's seal. Since the city's 825th anniversary in 1985, the building is once again the seat of the Mayor, after it had been out of use for almost a century. Some half-timbered constructions at the back were replaced by a modern building.

Beside the City Hall, the baroque facade of the city pharmacist's house was reconstructed in 1975 and two old sculptures of lions flank a stone bench in front of the house. The adjoining buildings have replaced old houses torn down in 1975 and were adapted to the proportions of the eighteenth century constructions. No. 11 houses the **City Information** office; sight-seeing tours start from there during the summer season.

At noon, a carillon on City Hall sounds the tune of an old popular song. The fountain on *Schlachtermarkt* by Stefan Horota (1980) refers to the old Mecklenburg folk song of »the parish priest's cow«.

The *Schlachtermarkt* [Butchers' Market], today a picturesque city square with flower and vegetable stands, was created in the late nineteenth century when a block was demolished. The *Schlachterstrasse* [Butchers' Street] alongside the square dates back to the thirteenth century, its buildings being mainly from the eighteenth and nineteenth centuries. Until the *Reichskris-*

tallnacht, when it was destroyed by fire under the Nazi regime, the lots occupied by Nos. 3 and 5 were the site of the Schwerin **Synagogue**. A memorial stone in the courtyard reminds of it, while house No. 5 is the see of the Jewish communities in Mecklenburg and Schwerin. The refurbished houses Nos. 9–13 include the *Alt Schweriner Schankstuben* restaurant, and **No. 17** is once again the seat of the Schwerin Free Masons in 1992.

The building on *Puschkinstrasse* **No. 34** walling off the square to the north is also part of the *Schlachtermarkt* area. Its two-storey side wing built in 1574 is the oldest profane building that has been preserved. The baroque house adjoining perpendicularly with its beautiful rococo door was built in the early eighteenth century and – after being an inn and a hotel for more than 200 years – is now used as an administrative building.

The fountain on Schlachtermarkt square.

The Cathedral

In the immediate proximity of the Market, the Cathedral (Dom) stands out as the only medieval construction of Schwerin. Its position within the city is due to Henry the Lion's decision to let the highest elevation of the city – then under construction – to the Chapter.

Presumably in 1160 – the year of the city's foundation – Bishop Benno had formally moved the existing Mecklenburg bishopric to Schwerin in order to ensure the presence of the Church in the developing political and economic centre of the county. Apart from the later Franciscan Church destroyed soon after the Reformation, the Cathedral is the only ecclesiastical construction from the Middle Ages. Therefore it also had to serve as the parish church.

The first construction was consecrated in 1171, but no information on its construction has been preserved. Already in the outgoing twelfth century a new construction was started on the same site that was to represent the growing importance of the Schwerin diocese. The cathedral of nearby *Ratzeburg* served as an example, as this late Romanesque brick construction was exemplary for many other churches. Until the consecration in 1248 or 1249, a brick basilica was erected with three naves, a transept, an apsis in the chancel and an outset tower that seems to have been planned as part of a two-tower facade. This construction has not been preserved either, but fragments of architecture and a comparison with the spire torn down in 1889 allow the deduction of its shape. The **Paradise Gate** preserved in the southern tower basement in its early ogival style is the oldest piece of architecture in Schwerin, dating back to 1240.

The great income that the pilgrims to the relic of the Holy Blood had brought to the city (the latter having been on show since 1222) catered for the idea of yet another new Cathedral in 1270. Only the latest in style, though, would be used for the reconstruction of the Schwerin cathedral, and the latest in style meant the French and Flemish style as represented in the churches of *Lübeck* (*St. Marien*) and *Stralsund* (*St. Nikolai*). Apart from the basilica-shaped floor plan, these churches are distinguished by their row of chapels surrounding the chancel.

Around 1270, this new construction was started from its eastern end. Five chapels connected to the hallway around the chancel were built, with the chancel closing the three-vaulted middle nave. The side naves open into a hallway. Until 1327, the chancel part and the nave on the eastern side of the monumental transept were completed. Then the preceding construction had to be dismantled in order to proceed with the construction. In 1347, the side walls of the main naves and the pillars were finished, while the construction of the vaults was not completed before the mid-fifteenth century. Meanwhile the financial power of the diocese had begun to slacker, so the planned spire could not be built. Today's Victorian tower was not built before 1889–93 to a design by architect Georg Daniel.

The interior of the cathedral is determined by its steep proportions resulting from the height of the central nave vaults of 28 metres, from the wall rising vertically without visual breaks and from the colouring. The colouring of the nave is mainly whitewash with only a few coloured accents. It was made in

View of the chancel of Schwerin Cathedral through the central nave.

1981–88 based upon the results of a thorough research of the original painting of the Cathedral.

Unlike in other churches in Northern Germany, only few traces of medieval figural painting have been preserved in Schwerin Cathedral. These cover the vaults and the walls of **Maria-Himmelfahrts-Kapelle** [St. Mary's Ascension Chapel] in the nave on the northern side of the transept. The vault paintings were made around 1340 and represent medallions with the symbols of the Evangelists, Kings, Prophets and other scenes, as well as various creeper designs. A few outline sketches mostly with scenes from the Bible in red chalk from the late fourteenth century are visible on the north side, while the frescoes covering the sketches have been lost. Over the inside of the Market gate, a picture of **St. Christopher** was uncovered in 1988.

Unfortunately, the Cathedral has preserved only very little of its original equipment. We cannot but guess at what was lost of the Catholic treasure during the Reformation: presumably dozens of altar retables and sculptures, gold and silver work, textiles, stained glass windows etc. In the following centuries further works of art were lost through natural degradation, theft, plundering etc., and as late as 1815 and 1867/68 parts of the old Renaissance and baroque furniture were removed for aesthetic reasons, for the church furniture was to match its medieval exterior. Therefore, neo-gothic furniture was installed: the choir stalls and the pulpit, the seats in the naves, the western choir as well as the **organ**. The latter is a four-manual work with 84 registers and some 6,000 pipes – the largest organ in Mecklenburg, built in 1871 at the *Weissenfels* workshops by Friedrich Ladegast. No less a person than Albert Schweitzer fought for its preservation. In 1988, a general restoration was completed and ever since the instrument presents itself at services and concerts with an almost original sound.

The chancel houses the *Lettner* altar, called **Kreuzaltar** or (in honour of the donator) *Loste* altar. It is a late medieval (ogival) winged altarpiece with a stone centrepiece from 1440 in the shrine. The latter shows the crucifixion scene and connected topics from the Passion, and several figures carved in wood, dating from 1495. The two sculptures in the centre part are the Cathedral's patrons, St. Mary and St. John the Evangelist. In front of the Main altar we find the new altar table consecrated in 1988 above a floor symbolizing a labyrinth, in the background of the chancel there is a neo-gothic **altar retable**, dated 1844, with a painting of the Crucifixion scene by Gaston Lenthe. The pillars are decorated with four **wooden epitaphs** from the sixteenth century commemorating the Mecklenburg dukes. The beam spanning the triumphal arch on the entrance to the chancel carries the medieval crucifixion group from the destroyed St. Mary's church of *Wismar*.

When visiting the chapels surrounding the chancel you will notice the beautiful **tomb** of Duke Christoph and his wife, created in 1595 at the Anvers workshops of Robert Coppens. Its lower part is decorated with alabaster

Tomb of Duke Christoph and his wife.

reliefs of biblical scenes and of arms, while the upper part consists of a life-sized representation of the pair kneeling. Some of the windows above the tomb include **glass paintings** from the seventeenth century, while the stained glass windows in the three central chapels date from the mid and late nineteenth century. These chapels house the **sarcophaguses** of members of the ducal family. Grand Duke Paul Friedrich, under whose rule Schwerin began to change its exterior in the second quarter of the nineteenth century, had asked to be buried in the former Sacred-Blood-Chapel. Therefore, G.A. Demmler started to prepare the central chapel for the funeral in 1842, the lateral chapels being later adapted to the style of the first.

In the Middle Ages, the Dukes of Schwerin were buried here, too, they are remembered by some relics of frescoes on the pillars of the chancel. The southernmost chapel contains a crypt with sarcophaguses from the sixteenth and seventeenth centuries, above them the great marble vase. Remains of medieval glass paintings from the fourteenth and fifteenth centuries are displayed in the window. The facing pillar includes the epitaph to Duchess Helena, cast in bronze in 1527 by Peter Vischer in Nuremberg, an early Renaissance work of high quality. Under the pulpit in the southern part of the transept – near Market gate – we find a **bronze group** originally from *Wolde* near *Stavenhagen*, showing the crucified Lord and Mary Magdalen, created in 1854 by the Dresden sculptor Ernst Rietschel.

The Ascension chapel in the transept contains the Cathedral's **baptismal font**, a bronze work dated from around 1400. Not far from this on both sides of the door leading to the cloister we find two brass plates as epitaphs to four bishops from the von Bülow family, created in Flanders workshops in the fourteenth century. Both plates show – besides the images of the dead – a number of biblical and allegorical figures and scenes, among them on the larger plate a drinking scene and a rape as the symbols of evil. The representations of the Kings and Prophets with their musical instruments (most of them unknown today) deserve your attention.

The Christmas Window in the western wall of the southern Tower Hall should be pointed out, it was made in 1848 and originally adorned the window above the western entrance to the cathedral. Two eighteen-armed chandeliers from 1616 and 1641 hang from the Cathedral's vault.

The ascent to the **tower gallery** – over fifty yards high – is more than just commendable. Climbing the 200 steps is amply repaid by the wonderful view from above: To the southeast you can overlook Market square and the Theatre, the Castle and the *Grosser Dreesch* in the background, to the east you can see Lake Schwerin; in the north you will see the *Schelfstadt* area, in the north-west you may look over the *Pfaffenteich* to the Railway Station, the *Hotel Stadt Schwerin* and the residential area of *Lankow*. In the west you can see St. Paul's church, the Court of Justice building and the quarters around *Wittenburger Strasse*. Finally, the south shows you Lake *Ostorf* and the industrial area of southern Schwerin with the huge granary at *Wüstmark* in the background.

Next to the Cathedral's northern side we find the **cloister**. The four sides of the cloister were built in the fourteenth and fifteenth centuries and include two upper storeys, the northern side of the cloister serves as a pedestrian passage. The ground floor of the east wing houses the former chapter house, today St. Thomas' chapel. The interior is relatively new, made after a design by the Dresden sculptor Friedrich Press. The other parts are used by the Mecklenburg State Library.

☞ During the summer season, the Cathedral is open Mon–Fri 1000–1300 and 1400–1700, Sat 1100–1700, Sun 1200–16.00. Outside the season: Mon–Fri 1100–1200 and 1400–1500, Sat 1100–1300 and 1400–1600, Sun 1200–1500.

The Old Garden from the Castle Tower.

The Old Garden

This square on the outskirts of the Castle area is sometimes called Schwerin's »Best Room«. Its name recalls the gardens present here in the seventeenth and eighteenth centuries that became the Old Garden (*Alter Garten*) when the new Castle Gardens were built. In 1834, the area was enlarged to the south by filling up part of the Castle Lake and the semicircle which still exists was planted with lime trees to round off the area. This is where the **Victory Column** (*Siegessäule*) was erected in 1874 to celebrate Germany's victory over France in the 1870/71 campaign.

The oldest house on the square is the half-timbered **Altes Palais** palace on *Schlosstrasse* corner, built in 1791 and enlarged eight years later. For many years it served as the widows' residence to the Dukes of Mecklenburg. In front of it we find the **Kollegiengebäude**, later called »*Regierungsgebäude I*«, the Government and Meetings Building on *Schlosstrasse* that in 1825–34 replaced the Franciscan monastery torn down during the Reformation. It was the first major construction by 19 year old G.A. Demmler in Schwerin, its classicist shape recalling the buildings of his teacher Karl Friedrich Schinkel.

Mecklenburg State Theatre at the Old Garden

Five allegoric figures ornate the roof, symbolizing the ruling powers. From 1890 to 1892, a second building was added by Georg Daniel.

Georg Daniel also designed the construction that leaves the most notable mark on the Old Market: The Mecklenburg State Theatre was built in 1882–86 in Italian Renaissance style on the same site where its ill-fated predecessor by Demmler had stood. Only the audience hall with its rich rococo-style stucco decoration has been preserved, the other rooms were »purified« in the 1960s. Since 1977, however, a reconstruction of the old interior is under way and has been completed in several areas such as the side foyer and the so-called »Flotow Chamber«.

The northern square front is occupied by the **State Museum**. This late classicist building designed by Hermann Willebrand, one of Demmler's collaborators in the construction of the Castle, was erected in 1877–82. At first it housed the collection of paintings and showed the rich trasure of seventeenth century Dutch masters. Today, the museum also includes coins, engravings and etchings, and a collection of some 10,000 works of artistic craftsmanship such as porcelaine, glass, arms and old furniture.

☞ The museum at the Old Garden is open Tue 1000–2000, Wed–Sun 1000–1700. Guided tours: Sun 1100, Wed 1500 and on demand. The museum has a shop and a cafeteria.

The steamers of the »White Fleet« on Lake Schwerin.

Just a few steps from the Museum we find the wharf where the boats of the **Weisse Flotte** [White Fleet] start for round-trips on the lake during the season. Ferry services to *Zippendorf, Muess* and to *Kaninchenweder* island are available.

The Castle

This many-towered construction, sited dreamily on an island in the southern part of Lake Schwerin, is the most visited monument of the city and doubtless one of its landmarks. The flat island bearing today's Castle is also the place where the city's history began. The main fortification of the Slavic Obotrite tribe was one of the main goals of Henry the Lion's 1160 campaign into the territory that was later to be Mecklenburg. Destroyed by its defenders, the **fortress** was rebuilt by its German conquerors and became the seat of the governor, and from 1167 of the count. In 1358, the Dukes of Mecklenburg decided to live at the Castle, and by the late sixteenth century it took more the shape of a palace than of a fortress. In 1553–55, Duke Johann Albrecht I had the eastern parts of the castle rebuilt on the occasion of his marriage to a Prussian princess, transforming them into comfortable living quarters. In 1560, a Protestant **chapel** was inserted. Further rebuilding took place in the seventeenth and eighteenth centuries.

When transferring his residence from *Ludwigslust* back to Schwerin in 1837, Grand Duke Paul Frederick considered the old castle to be unsuitable to live in. He began to build a palace on the Old Garden. When his successor Frederick Franz II came to the throne in 1842, the latter saw a chance to underline the rulers' descendance from the last Obotrite leader Niklot by refurbishing the old Castle. He commissioned his court architect Georg Adolph Demmler with the redesigning of the Castle. Gottfried Semper who built the Dresden Arts Gallery and Opera, and Friedrich August Stieler – who redesigned Berlin's Royal Palace – were also invited to participate. However, only Demmler's third proposal, incorporating some impressions he had taken from *Chambord Castle* on the river *Loire*, met with the Grand Duke's approval.

After the necessary dismantling of the old castle from 1843 to 1845, sparing only the Renaissance wings on the lakeside, the Castle was built in 1845–1847. In the middle of the construction work, Demmler was dismissed for having played a part in the political uprisings of 1848/49 and replaced by Stäler from Berlin, who altered his adversary's design of the city front. He designed a new domed solution, a figure programme over the main entrance and he rearranged the Court of Honour. In May 1857, the solemn inauguration took place, and the court composer Friedrich von Flotow composed an opera for the occasion.

When visiting the Castle you should start at the **main gate**. From the Court of Honour you can see the statues of counts and dukes on the city front, above them the mounted monument of the ancestor of the Dukes of Mecklenburg, the Obotrite prince Niklot killed in the 1160 war. Here is also the main access to the rooms occupied by the Mecklenburg-Vorpommern State Council. The parliament elected in the first free elections after the political changes hat its first solemn session here on October 26, 1990. Through the **Schlossgarten** [Castle Gardens] you reach the northwestern corner bastions with the tiny Tea House clinging to it like a swallow's nest. Left of it, the neo-gothic chancel of the **Castle Chapel** comes into sight, built in 1855 by the Cologne cathedral architect Zwirner.

After passing the **Felsengrotte** [Rock Grotto] you reach the colonnade at the orangery court with a good view of the main tower, the Great New House and the Bishop's House. The two buildings on the sides of the tower are examples of the Mecklenburg Renaissance architecture of the mid-sixteenth century with their typical terracotta ornaments. The terracotta tiles were made by Statius von Düren from *Lübeck*. The medallions representing rulers from the Antique and the Renaissance as well as the ornamental tiles have been replaced by copies in the nineteenth century.

The **orangery** rests at the foot of the main tower. Its court, surrounded by the colonnade, was an adequate setting for theatre and concert performances. Behind the great plane tree that shades the small court with the seashell

Gable detail with the ornate chimney pots and terracotta ornaments.

fountain, the palace – in Dutch Renaissance style – rises above the Castle Church. The **southern wing** facing the gardens, with its passage from the courtyard is the main access to the Castle Museum. The balcony above the *Jägerportal* [Hunters' Gate] shows two life-size herald figures by the sculptor Albert Wolff. South-west of here we find the **Lake Wing** facing a bronze monument of Grand Duke Paul Friedrich by Christian Daniel Rauch. It was erected in 1849 at the Old Garden to commemorate the Grand Duke during whose albeit short reign (1837–42) Schwerin grew from a small provincial city into a well-designed fashionable and spacious residence with numerous new public buildings.

The Castle has been owned by the State since World War I and was used as a museum from 1920 to 1945. After World War II, the Castle served as an administration and school building, the rooms not being open to the public prior to 1974.

The historical halls and rooms that have been refurbished hitherto are worth visiting. They form part of the **Schloss Museum**. At the **Beletage** floor, the former dining hall, the Red Audience, the tea room, the Flower Room in the tower, the Winter Hall, and the Sylvester Gallery are open to the public. All these rooms that made up part of the Grand Ducal family's living rooms, stand out with their solid furniture, their rare wood panelling on the walls, their inlaid floors, their stucco and carved ceiling beams.

The Throne Hall on the Festive Floor.

The rooms on the **Festive Floor** above have a more official character: the Throne Hall, the Ancestors' Gallery, the Castles' Gallery and the Library. The **Throne Hall** is very luxuriously equipped, for here noble materials like *Carrara* marble, gilt stucco and colourful frescoes and paintings are combined to form a noble entity. When one third of the castle was destroyed by fire in 1913, the similarly furnished but considerably larger Festival Hall was a victim of the flames. In the **Ancestors' Gallery,** the Mecklenburg rulers

The Ancestors' Gallery with the portraits of the Mecklenburg Dukes.

from the fourteenth to the eighteenth century are presented in period paintings. The Castles' Gallery parallel to the former shows the most important castles and palaces in the possession of the former grand-ducal family, among them *Güstrow*, *Ludwigslust* and the *Palais* at Rostock.

The »**Malerei in Mecklenburg**« Gallery of Mecklenburg Painting is part of the museum, displaying paintings from the eighteenth to the twentieth century and is situated in the former nursery rooms on the first intermediate floor.

☞ The Museum is open April through October Tue–Sun 1000–1800; October through April Tue–Sun 1000–1700. On show: the representative halls and the art collections on Beletage and Festive floors, as well as the Gallery of Mecklenburg Painting. Guided tours are available.

The Castle Gardens

Before or after visiting the Castle, a tour through the Castle Gardens is recommended (actually, there is a Castle Garden – *Burggarten* – and a Palace Garden – *Schlossgarten*). The **Castle Garden** is the garden area created in 1856 on Castle Island, interesting above all for its harmony of architecture, gardening and lakescape. Besides dendrological specialities, among them a huge *Gingko biloba*, the view on lake Schwerin is well worth a visit, and the best viewing point is just above the grotto. You will see the *Marstall* Stables across Castle Bay as well, and a rest under the shady trees is very peaceful. If you leave Castle Island by the rear bridge you will enter the **Palace Garden**. Although based upon older designs, the baroque garden's aspect is due mainly to the French architect and garden designer Jean L. Legay, who redesigned the garden in 1748–56. The garden's main axis is determined by the **Kreuzkanal** canal, the northern part of which was filled up in favour of the bower. 14 stone **sculptures** of ancient gods and of the four seasons are set up on the banks. They were made around 1720 in the workshops of the Dresden sculptor Balthasar Permoser and replaced by copies in 1960.

The **bronze monument** in the front part of the garden was cast in 1893 by the sculptor Ludwig Brunow from Berlin and commemorates Grand Duke Frederick Franz II. The southern part of the garden consists mainly of the **Cascades** that date back to the baroque period, too. Although set into the incline, at that time no water-works were installed. The small **pavilion** near the canal was actually built as a cafe in 1818 and still serves the same purpose.

In the nineteenth century, the garden was enlarged to the south, now designed as a landscape garden by Peter Joseph Lenné (1849). In the same year, the **Grünhausgarten** [Greenhouse Garden] was given its large **greenhouse** as a centre. A marble statue of Grand Duchess Alexandrine by Hugo Berwald was inaugurated in 1907. On the outskirts of the Greenhouse Garden you will find the **Schleifmühle** [Grinding Mill]. The latter is a half-timbered house reconstructed in 1985 with a huge water-wheel. Since the eighteenth century, stone from local quarries has been cut and polished here for various architectural purposes, such as tables, window sills and mantlepieces. As a technical museum, the *Schleifmühle* is part of Schwerin's Historical Museum.

☞ The *Schleifmühle* is open from April 1 through November 30 Tue–Sun 0900–1700. In addition to the mill's interior, an exhibition informs about the history of mills in general. Occasionally the mill can be seen in operation, group tours are available on appointment.

At the Castle Gardens.

The historic Grinding Mill.

Schlosstrasse

The Old Garden is connected to *Marienplatz* (St. Mary's Square) – the main traffic node of the city – by busy *Schlosstrasse* (Castle Street), today part of Schwerin's pedestrian zone. Near the castle there is a wealth of buildings created in the nineteenth and early twentieth centuries for all kinds of public administration. Besides the Government Building mentioned above you can see another construction by G. Daniel, similar in style but dating only from the late nineteenth century. This building is connected to the older Government Building by a covered hallway nicknamed »*Beamtenlaufbahn*« (Officers' runway – a pun, for *Laufbahn* in German means both »runway« and »career«). Under it you get a first glance of the *Mecklenburgisches Landeshauptarchiv* State Archive, built in 1909–11 by Paul Ehmig. It consists of two parts, the administration building and the high storage house and is entirely built upon posts driven into the ground.

Towards the north, the *Ritterstrasse* [Knights' Street] leads away from *Schlosstrasse,* and on it we find one of the most beautiful examples of baroque brick construction: House **No. 14/16** was built around 1770 presumably to plans by the Ludwigslust Court Architect Johann Joachim Busch. At about the same time, the facade of **No. 10** was redesigned in a rococo manner. The facade was restored to its original condition a couple of years ago, although the half-timbered building as such could not be preserved. **No. 12**

The Government Building, engraving by J. Gottheil.

is a former hotel built in 1844 by Demmler »for noble foreigners«. Today it serves as an administration building just like the former »*Nordischer Hof*« Hotel right across the street on **Nos. 7–11**.

On the southern part of *Schlosstrasse* street you will find the Catholic **St. Anna's church**, a baroque construction by Johann Cornelius Barca, consecrated in 1795 as the first Catholic church in Mecklenburg after the Reformation. Its interior has conserved only part of the original furniture, the aisle with its vault was extended to the east in 1983–85 and a chapel was added in the basement.

☞ If the main entrance is closed you should try the parish house in *Klosterstrasse* 13. The hours of service are to be found in the showcase near the entrance.

In front of the church you will find the *Schusterstrasse* [Shoemakers' Street], a few steps to the left there is the traditional restaurant **Weinhaus Uhle** (*Schusterstrasse* Nos. 13–15) with its old-fashioned guest room from 1905. In *Buschstrasse* street, some 60 yards to the west, we find the half-timbered cottage **No. 15,** a beautiful example of Schwerin's living quarters around 1700.

Half-timbered house at Buschstrasse No.15.

Grosser Moor

The *Grosser Moor* street connects *Puschkinstrasse* and *Werderstrasse*. The Riding Hall of the **Marstall** stables, built in 1838–43 by Demmler, is a beautiful streetside building on the eastern side. It detracts a little from the rather sober and poor new constructions that replaced older half-timered houses on the east side of the street in 1975. Although in poor shape, these buildings in the area between the Theatre, the *Grosser Moor* and *Burgstrasse* streets were among the oldest structures in the city and added a special flair

74

to this area, a flair lost with their destruction and replacement.

The palace-like half-timbered building at **No. 30** on the eastern side dates from the eighteenth century and used to be an Officers' Club. Today it is used by the city administration. No. 36 houses the Theatre Cafe, No. 38 is the seat of the **Historical Museum**. This building was created around 1720 and lately restored to its original condition. Since 1985 it has housed the museum's collections on the history of the city. A late classicist room with a renewed wall painting is used for displaying the interior of an early nineteenth century living room. Presently, the house is being redesigned as a place of historical research and exhibition.

☞ The Historical Museum is open Tue–Sun 1000–1800. The city history permanent exhibition is due to be reopened in October 1995.

Puschkinstrasse No.17.

The Schelfstadt

This part of the city is unique in more than one way. It is bordered to the west by the *Pfaffenteich* lake, to the south by *Friedrich* and *Burgstrasse* streets, to the east by *Werderstrasse* and to the north by *Ziegelinnensee* lake and *Knudtstrasse*. From 1705 to 1832 it was a town in its own right, independent from Schwerin. And it does differ remarkably both in the city layout and in its buildings.

In the Middle Ages, the *Schelfe* (i.e. »flat island«) belonged to the bishopric domain and had but a fishermen's village and a church. Later, Schwerin citizens settled there in the southernmost part, that is, in today's *Pfaffen, Puschkin, Fischer* and *Münzstrasse* streets area. In 1705, Duke Frederick William decreed that the *Neustadt Schwerin* (New City) should be built on the *Schelfe* island and should be open for religious refugees from France as

Half-timbered houses on Schelfmarkt square.

well as for craftsmen and traders from other countries. The Duke was interested in increasing his country's economic prosperity. In the same year, the development project was started, planned by the Captain Engineer Jacob Reutz. He had developed a pure baroque layout with streets intersecting at right angles and proposed half-timbered two-storey buildings on the main streets, as well as single-storey buildings on the lanes. He had even drawn up master plans for the houses, and the Duke supported the development with tax reductions, by granting building material etc. Therefore, the **half-timbered buildings** still play a major role in the quarter's exterior.

Reutze's special talent, however, became evident in the centre of the Schelfstadt, where he completed the main square aligning the church and the oblong rectangular square to form one of the most beautiful ensembles in Schwerin. The houses at *Puschkinstrasse* Nos. 1–11 and on *Lindenstrasse* streets, however, only partially date back to the early and later eighteenth century, some of them were built as late as 1857 (the neo-gothic corner house at *Linden* and *Puschkinstrasse*) or even 1905 (the *Art Deco* building at No.1 *Puschkinstrasse*). They have their own architectural qualities and integrate well with the half-timbered constructions on *Schelfmarkt* like the pharmacy or the double house at No. 3/4. Between them we find the former **City Hall,**

Schelfkirche church

built in 1776. Another very attractive building is the corner house at **Tauben-strasse No. 19**, dominating the northbound *Schelfstrasse* street like a gateway.

From a historical point-of-view, the most important building is the *Schelfkirche* church, also by Reutz. It was begun in 1708, is a cross-shaped brick building with a spire to the west and reintroduced pure brick constructions in Mecklenburg after a break of over 150 years. In this case, some ornaments were made from sandstone. After Reutz's death in 1710, the architecture theoretician L.Ch. Sturm surveyed the construction work. Some members of the Mecklenburg ducal family are buried under the nave, among them also Sophie Luise (died 1735), third wife of the first Prussian King Frederick I.

On *Puschkinstrasse* you will find some interesting buildings, such as the beautiful half-timbered house at No. 17, with its remarkable rococo door, or the former **Neustädtisches Palais** (No. 19), greatly changed in the nineteenth century, another gabled half-timbered house (No. 20) and the renowned winery *Wöhler* on *Fischerstrasse* that has been closed for years.

Pfaffenteich And Paulsstadt

With some 32 acres, the *Pfaffenteich* lake northwest of the centre is the smallest of all Schwerin lakes, and the only artificial one. It was created as a mill basin presumably around 1160 to provide the necessary water supplies for the county mill in the city and to protect the city's northwestern side. In order to achieve this aim, today's *Spieltor* dam was built across the *Aubach* creek, creating an artificial lake outside the city, for the town ended at today's *Mecklenburg* and *Arsenalstrasse* intersection, just where the *Haus der Kultur* is situated. Around 1840, when an extension of the city had become necessary and the area to the west of *Pfaffenteich* was considered, Demmler proposed to use the lake as a given element in the city design. The south and west banks were elevated and the first constructions were built after the western shoreline had been straightened.

The houses in today's *Karl-Marx-Strasse* were built between 1840 and 1865, the first being the **Arsenal** in Tudor style by Demmler (1840–44). Simultaneously, the **Amtshaus** [Public Administration Building, Nos. 20/21] was built from plans by August Bartning. Several buildings were changed in their exterior in later decades, such as the traditional hotel »*Niederländischer Hof*« (No. 12/13). On the southern side of *Pfaffenteich*, we find the *Kommandantenhaus* [Commanders' House] by Demmler, dating back to 1840. Only a few yards from there stands the building of former *Stern's Hotel,* today's *Haus der Kultur.* The most famous among the hotel's guests was Richard Wagner, who watched the performance of his own works at the Theatre in

The Pfaffenteich ferry.

1873. After 1945, the *Kulturbund* cultural association took over the house that was to develop into a cultural centre for the whole of Mecklenburg. After a long period of restoration, it was reopened in 1989 as a lively art centre. Just in front, on *Arsenal* and *Mecklenburgstrasse* intersection, we find the yellow house where Demmler lived and died. He had received the site as a gift by Grand Duke Paul Friedrich and created the villa in 1842–44.

The eastern banks of *Pfaffenteich* lake were open for development only from 1865, hence there are only late nineteenth century buildings. On *Friedrich-strasse* corner there is the remarkable late classicist building of the Kücken Foundation (1868), the monument to the composer Friedrich Kücken by Ludwig Brunow (1885) on the strip of lawn in front of it commemorates the creator of many popular songs. Two buildings on *August-Bebel-Strasse* street recall sixteenth century Mecklenburg Renaissance court architecture with their *terracotta* decoration: the *Gymnasium Fridericianum* College of 1870 and the former *Kuetemeyer* Foundation of 1894, today the registrar's office. In front of the college a terrace carries a monument to the archeologist Heinrich Schliemann who is (wrongly) said to have frequented Schwerin's college but who was born at *Neubukow* some forty miles north of Schwerin

The Arsenal on Pfaffenteich.

on January 6, 1822. The city's first electricity plant on the north bank (dated 1904) is the latest example of neo-Renaissance architecture.

A ferry service crosses the 230 yards wide *Pfaffenteich*, a commodity for passers-by. You should not miss the view on the city, the Arsenal, the spires etc. from the water.

St. Paul's church is part of *Pfaffenteich* architectural setting. Its eastern parts can be seen alongside the Arsenal through *Moritz-Wiggers-Strasse* street. This most prominent neo-gothic church building in Mecklenburg was built in 1863–69 to a design by Theodor Krüger. The church has three naves of equal height, a transept, a polygonal chancel and a tower to the west. The interior has been preserved in its original shape. The chancel is fitted with a huge altar by one Pfannschmitt, with carved seats and multicoloured glass windows. On the western balcony we find one of the greatest organs the Schwerin company Friese ever built, and after being overhauled a few years ago it has been the main instrument of organ concerts. In the late nineteenth century, Johannes Brahms directed some concerts here, as his signature on the scores' cupboard shows.

☞   St. Paul's Church is open Sat–Sun 1100–1200 and 1300–1600.

Demmler's house and the »Haus der Kultur« on Arsenalstrasse.

Mecklenburgstrasse

Schwerin's most important business street begins on the southern bank of *Pfaffenteich* and has been a **pedestrian zone** since 1977. Just as you would not notice anything of the former tram and car traffic here, you will not be aware that you are walking on the former city borders – for centuries this was just a moat. Until the closure of the mill at *Schlosstrasse* and *Kloster-strasse* in 1853, the latter was supplied with water from the *Pfaffenteich* through a canal under today's street.

The numerous shops are of special interest for tourists, but you should pay some attention to the neo-Renaissance style **Main Post Office** of 1892–97 by Hake, and the slightly newer Telephone Office nearby. Between the two of them, you will have an imposing view of the Cathedral spire. On *Schmiedestrasse* street that extends eastward from the shopping centres you will find a singular example of older architecture in No. 15, dating back to 1700 with a rich facade on its *Bischofsstrasse* street front. The majority of the old buildings in this area, however, had already changed in the nineteenth century. A hundred yards further on there is lively *Helenenstrasse* going down to *Marienplatz* square, while the *Enge Strasse* [Narrow Lane] on the left really deserves its name.

After the *Schlosstrasse* crossing the street loses its boulevard character, the small square on the left is the bus station. Until a few years ago, this space was filled with apartment buildings that had to be torn down due to weak foundations on the marshes. The **Art-Déco houses** at Nos. 61–73 show signs of great neglect and call for refurbishment. From the **bus station** there are several interesting downtown bus lines, No. 15 will take you to the beautiful *Fauler See* area, to the Youth Hostel and to the Zoo.

Central Railway Station

Schwerin's Central Railway Station is situated to the northwest of the city centre, but the Market square can be reached within a 15 minutes' walk. Tram No.1 will take you to *Marienplatz* square if you'd rather not walk. The **station building** was constructed in 1888–90 by the Hamburg architect Möller. The administration building south of the tracks is ten years younger. Schwerin was connected to the Hamburg–Berlin line with the Schwerin–*Hagenow* branch in 1847.

On *Grunthalplatz* square in front of the station building you will find the »*Stadt Schwerin*« Hotel opened in 1972, a modern construction with 350 beds, at present closed for refurbishment. Right in front there are two more hotels, the »*Reichshof*« and the »*Hotel am Hauptbahnhof*«. The fountain in the centre of the square made in 1911 by Hugo Berwald symbolizes rescue from distress on sea. The centre can be reached through *Wismarsche Strasse* road, but the way down to the *Pfaffenteich* area is more commendable, where you will have a beautiful view over the wide lakeside to the high spire of the Cathedral.

Left: View of Schwerin's pedestrian zone at Mecklenburgstrasse.
Following pages: Schwerin from the south.

© Edition Temmen

0 km 5

Niendorf
Hohen Viecheln
Bad Kleinen
Vents
Döpe
NSG
Zick-husen
Flessenow
Lieps
Neu Schlagsc
Schweriner See
Lübstorf
Retgendorf
Klein Trebbow
Hundorf
Cambs
Seehof
Kirch-stücker See
Rampe
Kirch Stück
Wicken-dorf
Groß Medewege
Ziegel See
Cambser See
Warnitz
Medeweger See
Schweriner See
Leezen
Friedrichsthal
Lankow
Lewen-berg
Schelf-werder
Neumühle
Heidensee
Görslow
Lankower See
Schwerin
Werder-vorstadt
Kaninchen-werder
Go
Weststadt
Ziegel-werder
Görries
Ostorf
Fauler See
Zippendorf
Mueß
Pinnower See
Pinn
Ostorfer See
Gr. Dreesch
Krebsförden
Raben Steinfeld
Wüstmark
Consrade
Störwasserstraße
Peckatel
Sukow
Plate
Banzko

Ausflüge in die Umgebung

In The Surrounding Area

Zippendorf And Muess

In the early nineteenth century, Schwerin's citizens had discovered the little village of *Zippendorf* on the south banks of Lake Schwerin as a summer resort and as the destination for excursions. In 1865, a regular steamer service was introduced, in 1879 the first public bathing area opened, and between 1921 and 1977 the tram connected the village with Schwerin. Those who prefer walking could and can walk there using the promenade from the Castle Gardens. *Zippendorf*'s present aspect is due to a lot of construction activity in the early twentieth century, when several hotels, villas and boarding houses were built. Three half-timbered cottages from the nineteenth century still recall the place's 700 years of history as a peaceful village. In 1984, the trade unions of the former G.D.R. had a huge 1,000-bed resort hotel named after *Fritz Reuter* built in the centre. Today it is used as a hotel.

Today, *Zippendorf* is Schwerin's most popular local resort, with some 10,000 guests crowding its sandy beaches. Boat hire, sports facilities, restaurants and bars make up some of the attractions. There is a regular ferry service to Schwerin and to *Kaninchenwerder* island, where there is also a lakeside beach, beautiful woods, a viewpoint tower and the »*Seeklause*« restaurant. Since 1923, the island has been a nature preservation area.

Zippendorf in the mid-nineteenth century, engraving by J. Gottheil.

The Kunstkaten at Schwerin-Muess open-air museum.

Half an hour away from *Zippendorf* lies **Muess**, a small country village incorporated in 1936. It still bears its rural aspect, especially since having been declared as architectural monument in 1970, thus being spared any detrimental changes to the centre. The **Mecklenburgisches Volkskunde-museum – Freilichtmuseum Schwerin-Muess** open-air museum founded in the same year gives an insight into country life from the past. The most important building in the museum is a Lower German half-timbered house from the mid-seventeenth century, but the other buildings such as a country school, a blacksmith's and a shepherd's cottage deserve attention, too. The **Kunstkaten** [Art shed] dates back to 1800 and opened in 1977 as an exhibition site for the museum's large collections.

☞ The museum is open from May through October Wed–Sun 1000–1800. Guided tours on agreement.

The Lewitz Villages:
Consrade, Plate, Peckatel And Banzkow

South of Schwerin lie the *Lewitz* plains with the *Stör* river. This area is still intensively used for agricultural purposes (cattle, potatoes and corn). Its relatively big villages have preserved much of their original aspect despite the proximity of the big city. In **Consrade**, for instance, there is an old

Lifting bridge over the Stör river at Plate.

half-timbered church from the late sixteenth and early seventeenth centuries with a separate bell tower and beautiful old oaks in the churchyard. Neighbouring **Plate** has been a tax collecting station for the shipping business. The village church is a neo-gothic brick building from 1849. In the nearby fire brigade house of 1927 there is a small museum of fire-fighting, worth a visit (open on Saturdays and on request).

The two inns »*Störkrug*« and »*Leiwitzidyll*« near the landing bridge of the White Fleet on the *Störkanal* are very inviting, and beyond the bridge some older farmhouses preserve their thatched roofs, just like in the village of **Peckatel** with its early eighteenth century half-timbered church on the village green.

Banzkow, situated on the outskirts of *Waldlewitz,* is the last in the line of villages. A revolving bridge built around 1895 crosses the *Störkanal*, the last working example of its kind in the Schwerin area. The nearside locks were once of great importance for goods transport, today only sports boats pass through the gates. *Banzkow* is renowned for its beautiful »*Lewitz-Mühle*« inn, but it also has remarkable old farmhouses and a neo-gothic church worth visiting.

Schwerin's Innensee Lake

Whoever wants to get acquainted with Schwerin's Lakescape is invited to take half a day to walk along Schwerin's *Innensee* [Inner Lake] area.

You should start at the Castle Gardens, where there is a survey plan in front of the Greenhouse. Following the tarmacked **Franzosenweg** promenade along meadows and groups of trees you reach *Kalkwerder* with bathing facilities and an inn. On the right hand side there is the **Grosse Karausche** with numerous water lilies. After a short distance through a residential area with villas and after the »*Waldburg*« inn, the path leads to *Zippendorf* through two kilometres of woods. After crossing the village on the road parallel to the beach we take the shore path to **Muess**, passing the baths and a few boat houses. At *Muess* we reach the B 321 state road at the »*Muesser Bucht*« inn, then we take a left turn to the village centre to the *Alte Dorfstrasse* [Old Village street] which we leave halfway through for a small unpaved path on our right. This takes us to the **Reppiner Burgwall**, a small woody area with a beautiful viewpoint built in 1907 in romantic style. From there the path leads us along boat houses to the beginning of the *Störkanal* near the Ferry inn (»*Zur Fähre*«).

☞ During the season (May through September), you may take the steamer back to Schwerin Castle.

Over the road bridge of the B 321 – passing by the memorial for the victims of the *Sachsenhausen* Death March of May 1945 – we reach **Raben Steinfeld** on our left. On the right there is a forester's house in Swiss cottage style, facing it a shore path turns left. It leads to the village centre as does the main road. The village has some interesting neogothic villas from 1865 and the castle built for the Grand Duke in 1886/87 with a remarkable park. Beneath the park, the shore path leads through beautiful woods to *Görslow*. On the right hand side, the steep shore goes up some thirty yards, while on the left hand side the wide waterside exends to its maximum of four miles. From here there is not only a marvellous view over the lake to Schwein, a bathing area invites for a swim, too. For the return we recommend walking to *Raben-Steinfeld*, from where there are hourly buses back to town.

Raben Steinfeld memorial.

Schwerin's Aussensee Lake

The *Aussensee* [Outer Lake] is a frequently visited recreation area with several large camping sites. From Schwerin, you can reach the eastern banks on the B 104 road towards *Güstrow*, passing the *Werderholz* grove with its huge beeches and crossing the canal that connects the Inner and Outer Lakes at the »*Seewarte*« inn. Here, the two mile long *Paulsdamm* [Paul's dam] begins, built across the lake in 1842–44. At the village *Rampe* we turn left into the shore road, where there are numerous pretty bathing areas. After some three miles we reach **Retgendorf** with its large camping site in a very quiet area. The village's medieval brick church from the fourteenth century is worth visiting. Another camping site is at **Flessenow** farther north.

The road leads on to the **nature preservation area** near the *Döpe* pond. The pond is only five feet deep and surrounded by reeds and shrubs that offer an undisturbed home to many water birds. Beyond the railway line lies the village of **Hohen Viecheln** with a large three-naved brick church from around 1300 that contains numerous valuable pieces of church furniture and equipment. Either on the shore path or on the road you can reach **Bad Kleinen**. The path crosses the *Wallensteingraben* ditch cut in the sixteenth century as part of a planned shipping canal from Schwerin to *Wismar*. Schwerin's »secret central station« on the north shore of Lake Schwerin is a railway junction, the village *Kleinen* developing with the railway in the nineteenth century. It became a health resort and was allowed to add »Bad«, i.e. »Spa«, to its original name. Several inns along the shore are ideal for a rest.

The island of **Lieps** is still being used for agricultural production. From *Bad Kleinen* to *Lübsdorf* you should rather take the road, for the lakeside path is very bad. From **Lübsdorf** you may go on directly to Schwerin on the B 106, passing *Kirch Stück* and its medieval village church as well as the charming *Aubachtal* valley. If you turn left into the lakeside street you are rewarded with a wealth of beautiful views of the lake.

But before, there is the opportunity to take the road near the railway crossing to **Schloss Wiligrad** palace (two miles) that comes into view once you get out of the beechwood forest. It was built in 1896–1898 in Mecklenburg Renaissance style and houses the *Schloss Wiligrad* Arts association and its regular exhibitions. The castle is also the seat of the State Preservation Authority and of the **Archeological State Museum.**

Passing through **Alt-Lobstorf** and the farmers' village of *Hundorf* you will finally reach *Seehof.* The village was founded in 1838 as a typical manor village. It offers an international camping site, a restaurant and a bathing area. This village, too, is reached by the White Fleet's steamers.

The next village to follow is *Wickendorf,* already part of the city of Schwerin. Its houses have lost their traditional aspect due to the heavy modernization in the last few decades. The road to the right at the restaurant leads through the **Wickendorfer Moor** marshes to the »*Seewarte*« restaurant on Pauls Dam. Continuing towards Schwerin you pass by the *Carlshöhe* and *Wendenhof* quarters, the latter offering a fantastic view over *Ziegelsee* lake onto the city. It is the place where Erich Honecker had the luxurious *Frankenhorst* Hotel built. The city can be reached again via *Medwege* at the District Hospital.

View over Ziegelsee lake.

Excursions From Schwerin

Ludwigslust

Schwerin's sister town *Ludwigslust* is situated some 24 miles south on the B 106 and on the railway line to Berlin and Leipzig.

Ludwigslust developed as the residence of the Dukes of Schwerin where the village of *Klenow* had existed since the fourteenth century. The new town had to be made from scratch, for besides stony meadows and woods there was practically nothing. Water – so important for human life in general and for a **baroque residence** as a means of design in particular – had to be brought in via a canal from *Lewitz*, some 13 miles away. In 1764, the court moved to *Ludwigslust* from Schwerin after the first buildings of the new residence designed by Johann Joachim Busch had been completed. Busch had provided an avenue as longitudinal axis – today's *Schlosstrasse* – and a second axis between the Palace and the Church as the basic grid for city development.

By the year 1800, the greater part of the baroque residence was finished. In 1765–70, the **Schlosskirche** (palace church), today's parish church, was built. It is remarkable above all for its huge column porch and its aisle, its enormous altar painting and the richly decorated ducal stall. The **Palace**, a three-storeyed building with seventeen rows of windows, was completed between 1772 and 1776. The high attic is decorated with 40 figures larger than life-size and 16 ornamental vases, all from the workshops of Rudolph Kaltunger. Historical furniture, paintings by the Mecklenburg court painters as well as other works of excellent craftsmanship help to recreate the atmosphere of life in a court of the eighteenth and nineteenth centuries. The most representative of the halls is the **Goldener Saal** [Golden Hall]. Its rich decorations are from *papier mâché* and were created mostly at the local *papier mâché* manufactory. Until 1945, the palace remained the home of the Grand Ducal family, in later years it was used for various office purposes. Today, it is part of the Schwerin State Museum.

☞ Opening hours: April through October Tue–Sun 1000–1800, October through April Tue–Sun 1000–1700. Public guided tours daily at 1400.

With some 300 acres, the **Park** is the largest in Mecklenburg. It was created simultaneously with the palace. In the mid-nineteenth century, the park was redesigned by the famous garden architect Peter Joseph Lenné to form a **landscape garden** in English style, although incorporating some parts of the former baroque design. Several interesting buildings can be found in the

Ludwigslust palace.

park, such as St. Helen's Church (1803–09), the Swiss *chalet* (around 1780) with a restaurant, two memorials (early nineteenth century) and the water works. Since 1981, the park is being gradually reconstructed.

Much of the baroque city design has been preserved in *Schlosstrasse*, *Thälmann* and *Nummerstrasse* streets, but the classicist extension of 1810–35 has suffered from redesign, road construction and neglect in the past few years, only the area along *Kanalstrasse* remained mostly unchanged. Near the railway station there is the great complex of the Bethlehem foundation from the mid-nineteenth century, its older buildings and the church are in neo-gothic style.

At *Wöbbelin*, some five miles north of Ludwigslust on the B 106, there are interesting memorials for the German poet Theodor Körner and for the victims of *Reiherhorst* concentration camp. Körner, the author of very popular national poems, fell in a battle against the French on August 26, 1813, and was laid to rest under an old oak at *Wöbbelin*. His grave is topped by a cast iron monument from the Berlin Iron Foundry (1814).

A small memorial museum, the **Mahn- und Gedenkstätte Wöbbelin**, informs us about the anti-napoleonic liberation wars in Mecklenburg and about Körner's biography. It also commemorates the victims of the nearby *Reiherhorst* concentration camp, an outpost of *Neuengamme* camp. The

Wöbbelin memorial.

memorial's park was one of the cemeteries of *Reiherhorst* concentration camp. Over 10,000 detainees were brought to this camp in the last weeks of the War between February and May 1945, more than half of them died under the inhuman conditions at the camp. A sandstone relief by the sculptor Jo Jastram (1960) commemorates this cruel event.

☞ Opening hours of the memorial: April through October Tue–Sun 1000–1700, November through March Tue–Sun 1000–1600.

Neustadt-Glewe And The Friedrichsmoor

Neustadt-Glewe can be reached from Schwerin via the motorway A 241 (exit *Neustadt-Glewe*) or via the B 106 to *Wöbbelin* and from there via the B 191. The town is one of the most important historical places in Mecklenburg. Founded in the thirteenth century, it developed into an important **fortress** on the river *Elde*, parts of which are preserved to the present (museum, Youth Hostel). The baroque castle was built in the seventeenth and eighteenth centuries. Due to neglect in the past decades, its wonderful stucco ceilings by Italian masters cannot be visited at present. The town was reconstructed with **half-timbered houses** after a fire in 1728, the most beautiful of which are on *Rudolf-Breitscheid-Strasse*. *Neustädter See* lake near the city is the local summer resort with camping sites and beaches.

The fortress in Neustadt-Glewe.

Friedrichsmoor can be reached from *Neustadt-Glewe* by road on the B 191 to *Tuckhude* junction, from there via a country road (6 miles). The three-winged half-timbered Hunting Lodge of the Mecklenburg Dukes built around 1780 is situated in *Waldlewitz*, an area full of game, of which large areas are natural reserves today. A valuable **wallpaper** printed in Paris in 1815 is on show at the lodge, presenting five scenes of a deer hunt in the *Compiègnes* woods near Paris. It came from *Friedrichsthal* castle and is believed to be the only preserved copy. From 1969, the place was used for educational puposes, since 1991 it has a small hotel and restaurant with seminary facilities.

☞ Jagschloss Friedrichsmoor, 19306 Friedrichsmoor, Phone/Fax 038757/ 22413. The Lodge can be visited during the restaurant's opening hours.

From *Friedrichsmoor* you may return to Schwerin via *Goldenstedt* and from there via *Banzkow* or else on the B 106.

 Staatliches Museum Schwerin
Kunstsammlungen, Schlösser und Gärten

The Schwerin State Museum presents permanent and special exhibitions,
offers guided tours of the collections, lectures, museum pedagogics,
seminaries, concerts, film presentations, museum shops
and invites you to relax in its coffee-shops and restaurants.

Galeriegebäude	**Schloßmuseum**
Alter Garten 3	Lennéstr. 1
19055 Schwerin	19053 Schwerin
Phone 0385/592400	Phone 0385/525920
Opening hours:	Opening hours:
Tue 1000–2000	Apr 15–Oct 14 Tue–Sun 1000–1800
Wed–Sun 1000–1700	Oct 15–Apr 14 Tue–Sun 1000–1700

Schloß Ludwigslust	**Schloß Güstrow**
Schloßfreiheit	Franz-Parr-Platz 1
19288 Ludwigslust	18273 Güstrow
Phone 03874/28114	Phone 03843/5021
Opening hours:	Opening hours:
Apr 15–Oct 14 Tue–Sun 1000–1800	Apr 15–Oct 14 Tue–Sun 1000–1800
Oct 15–Apr 14 Tue–Sun 1000–1700	Oct 15–Apr 14 Tue–Sun 1000–1700

For information phone 0385/59240-0, fax 0385/563090

Travel Information

Tourist Information

Deutsche Bahn AG, Reiseauskunft, Phone 0385/565687
Fremdenverkehrsamt/Schwerin-Information, Am Markt 11,
Phone 0385/560931, Fax 0385/562739
Opening Hours: Mon–Fri 1000–1800, Sat 1000–1400
Guided tours, Phone 0385/555082
Room Service, Phone 0385/565123, Fax 0385/555094
Information and advice, publications about Schwerin and its surroundings,
ticket service for concerts, cultural and sports events, guided tours, room
reservation.

Boat Hire

Bootsverleih am Schloss, Bornhövedstr. 65a, Phone 0385/512440

Book Shops

Boulevard-Buchhandlung, Helenenstr. 6, Phone 0385/565689
Buchhandlung am Marienplatz, Goethestr. 105, Phone 0385/565877
Buchhandlung für Recht und Wirtschaft, Goethestr. 29,
Phone 0385/5500660
Buchhandlung Stirnberg, Hauptbahnhof, Phone 0385/568656
Marktbuchhandlung, Am Markt 13, Phone 0385/565976
Niels-Stensen-Buchhandlung, Schlosstr. 20, Phone 0385/565804
Schloss-Buchhandlung, Schlosstr. 26, Phone 0385/555063
Schweriner Antiquariat, Puschkinstr. 59, Phone 0385/562912

Breakdown Service

ADAC, Phone 0385/5574655
KFZ-Hilfsdienst, Phone 0385/49225

Cafés (selection)

Café am Boulevard, Schlosstr. 30, Phone 0385/563017
Lesecafé, Arsenalstr. 16, Phone 0385/5574792
Café Prag, Puschkinstr. 64, Phone 0385/565909
Café »Rothe« Puschkinstr. 14, Phone 0385/5571305
Eck-Café »Ulrike«, Wittenburgerstr. 42, Phone 0385/732038
Schlosscafé im Schlossmuseum Schwerin, Lennéstr. 1, Phone 0385/5252963
Schlossgartenpavillon am Kreuzkanal, Am Kreuzweg, Phone 0385/565186
Theatercafé, Grosser Moor 36, Phone 0385/561126

Camping Sites near Schwerin

Campingplatz Seehof, Lübstorfer Str., Phone 0385/512540
Campingplatz »Süduferperle« Lesingleener Str. 1, 19065 Raben Steinfeld,
Phone 03860/312
Camping- und Wassersportzentrum Retgendorf, Seestr. 24,
19067 Retgendorf, Phone 03866/340

Campingplatz »Anne«, 19073 Dümmer, Phone 03869/216
Campingplatz am Militzsee, 19069 Crivitz, Phone 03863/2734
Ferienzentrum Neukloster, Bützower Str., 23992 Neukloster,
Phone 038422/844

Car Hire

City-Trans, Gadebuscher Str. 189, Phone 0385/479672
Europcar InterRent, Grevesmühlener Str. 18, Phone 0385/41133
Hertz, Wittenburger Str. 116, Phone 0385/7851941
Sixt Budget, Lilienthal Str. 2-10, Phone 0385/614172

Churches

Lutheran: Evangelische Kirche, Oberkirchenrat, Münzstr. 8,
Phone 0385/5185-0; Services: Sun 1000, at the Cathedral also Sat 1800
Roman Catholic: Katholische Kirche, Bischöfliches Amt, Lankower Str. 14,
Phone 0385/4576-0

Cinemas

Capitol, Wismarsche Str. 126, Phone 0385/565991
Schauburg, Mecklenburgstr. 53, Phone 0385/565121

City Tours (by bus)

Petermännchen-Stadtrundfahrten GmbH, Am Wasserturm 5,
Phone/Fax 0385/716041

Coach Tours

Fa. Bährle, Wallstr. 60, Phone 0385/71553
Fa. Günther, Krösnitz 9, Phone 0385/71064

Emergency Services

Hospital: Poliklinik Schwerin, Gausstr. 1, Phone 0385/569598
Ambulance, Phone 0385/115
Fire Brigade, Phone 112

Hotels

Europa Hotel Schwerin, Werkstr. 209, Phone 0385/63400,
Fax 0385/6340666 (28 single/52 double)
Best Western Hotel Plaza, Am Grünen Tal/Hamburger Allee,
Phone 0385/34820, Fax 0385/341053 (3 single/75 double)
Hospiz am Pfaffenteich, Gausstr. 19, Phone 0385/83321 (12 double)
Hotel am Hauptbahnhof, Grunthalplatz 11-12, Phone 0385/565702,
Fax 0385/5574296 (9 single/20 double)
Hotel »An den Linden« Franz-Mehring-Str. 26,
Phone/Fax 0385/512084 (3 single/9 double)
Hotel »Neumühler Hof«, Neumühler Str. 45,
Phone/Fax 0385/719361 (7 single/7 double)
Hotel »Nordlicht«, Apothekerstr. 2, Phone 0385/558150,
Fax 0385/5574383 (2 single/3 double)
Hotel »Reichshof«, Grunthalplatz 15-17, Phone 0385/565798
(6 single/20 double)

Landhaus Schwerin, An der Chaussee 28, Phone 0385/868510
(3 single/6 double)
Hotel »Arte«, Dorfstr. 6, Schwerin-Krebsförden, Phone 0385/63450,
Fax 0385/6345100 (22 single/18 double)
Hotel »Fritz Reuter« Räthenweg, Schwerin-Zippendorf, Phone 0385/2930,
Fax 0385/211144 (100 single/339 double)
Strand-Hotel, Am Strand 13, Schwerin-Zippendorf, Phone 0385/213053,
Fax 0385/321174 (2 single/24 double)
Hotel-Restaurant »Zur Fähre«, Alte Crivitzer Landstr., Schwerin-Muess,
Phone 0385/213054, Fax 0385/212130 (10 single/10 double)
Hotel-Restaurant »Zur Muesser Bucht«, Muesser Bucht 1, Schwerin-Muess,
Phone 0385/64450-0, Fax 0385/64450-44 (5 single/15 double)
Hotel Dobler, Peckateler Str. 4, Schwerin-Raben Steinfeld,
Phone 03860/8011, Fax 03860/8006 (10 single/ 20 double)
Seehotel Frankenhorst, Frankenhorst 5, Schwerin-Wickendorf,
Phone 0385/555071, Fax 0385/555073 (4 single/11 double)

Lost and Found

Fundbüro, Grosser Moor 2-6, Phone 0385/559223

Museums / Cultural institutions

Galerie am Pfaffenteich, Arsenalstr. 14, Phone 0385/5571713
Haus der Kultur, Kulturamt, Mecklenburgstr. 2, Phone 0385/592380
Historisches Museum Schwerin, Verwaltung und stadtgeschichtliche Ausstellung, Grosser Moor 38, Phone 0385/560971, Tue–Sun 1000–1800. Exhibitions about the city's history and special exhibitions at three venues. The city history permanent exhibition at Grosser Moor is scheduled to be reopened in October 1995.
Neues Gebäude am Markt, Am Markt 1, Phone 0385/562704,
Di–So 10–18 Uhr
Schweriner Schleifmühle, Schleifmühlenweg 1, 19061 Schwerin, Phone 0385/562751. Open April 1 through November 30, Tue–Sun 0900–1700.
Mecklenburgisches Volkskundemuseum – Freilichtmuseum Schwerin-Muess, Alte Crivitzer Landstr. 13, Phone 0385/213011, May through October Tue–Sun 1000–1800. The 16 reconstructed historical buildings at the open-air museum offer an insight into former peasant life in Mecklenburg.
Staatliches Museum Schwerin – Kunstsammlungen, Schlösser und Gärten, Alter Garten 3, Phone 0385/592400, Tue 1000–2000, Wed–Sun 1000–1700.
The Schwerin State Museum with the *Galeriegebäude* at the Old Garden and the museums at Schwerin, Güstrow and Ludwigslust castles is the largest art museum in Mecklenburg-Vorpommern.
The *Galeriegebäude* shows one of the largest German collections of Dutch and Flemish painting of the seventeenth century as well as medieval art from Mecklenburg, German painting from the Renaissance to the present and paintings by Jean Baptiste Oudry. Furthermore, it houses the engravings cabinet and collections of craftsmans' works.

Schlossmuseum Schwerin, Lennéstr. 1, Phone 0385/5252920, April through October Tue–Sun 1000–1800, October through April Tue–Sun 1000–1700. Representative rooms and art collections at Beletage and Festive floors, Gallery »Malerei in Mecklenburg«. Further extensions are due.

Sternwarte observatorium, Weinbergstr. 17, Phone 0385/512844, open Tue/Wed/Thu 0930 Uhr; Mon/Wed/Thu/Sat/Sun 1430, Fri 1900 with observations

Naturschutzstation Zippendorf, Am Strand 9, Phone 0385/213052

Police

Polizeidirektion Schwerin, Amtstr. 21-24, Phone 0385/5180-0

Polizeiinspektion Schwerin Mitte, Schlosstr. 10, Phone 0385/53930

Post Office

Direktion Schwerin, Mecklenburgstr. 4-6, Phone 0385/5710-0

Public Libraries and Archives

Mecklenburgische Landesbibliothek, Am Dom 2, Phone 0385/565197

Stadtbibliothek, Wismarsche Str. 144, Phone 0385/59019-0

Mecklenburgisches Landeshauptarchiv, Graf-Schack-Allee 2, Phone 0385/555411

Stadtarchiv, Platz der Jugend 12-14, Phone 0385/559286

Restaurants and Inns

Alt Schweriner Schankstuben, Schlachtermarkt 9-13, Phone 0385/565114

Am Stadttor, Lischstr. 3, Phone 0385/569744

Charivary, Wittenburger Str. 50, Phone 0385/734055

Einheit, Schlossgartenallee 38, Phone 0385/561332

Elefant, Goethestr. 39, Phone 0385/565703

Friesenhof, Mecklenburgstr. 2, Phone 0385/5570155

Gastmahl des Meeres, Grosser Moor 5, Phone 0385/565935

Gewölbe-Restaurant, Am Markt 1, Phone 0385/565166

Jagdhaus Schelfwerder, Güstrower Str. 109, Phone 0385/561216

Kochs Bier- und Weinstuben, Lennéstr. 2-4, Phone 0385/5574891

Primavera (Hotel Plaza), Am Grünen Tal/Hamburger Allee, Phone 0385/34820

Rasthof zum Goldenen Reiter, Puschkinstr. 44, Phone 0385/565036

Ritterstube, Ritterstr. 3, Phone 0385/565240

Seewarte, Paulsdammer Weg 2, Phone 0385/561554

Strandperle, Am Strand 14, Phone 0385/213263

Restaurant Weinhaus Uhle, Schusterstr. 15, Phone 0385/562956

Werderecke, Werderstr. 3, Phone 0385/562160

Zum Mecklenburger, Puschkinstr. 81, Phone 0385/564067

Restaurants, international cuisine

Brinkama's Restaurant (Italian), Lübecker Str. 33, Phone 0385/5507544

Restaurant »Peking Ente« (Chinese), Phone 0385/5507427

Restaurant Hellas (Greek), Bischofstr. 3, Phone 0385/563015

Restaurant Sparta (Greek), Schlossgartenallee 38, Phone 0385/561332

Ships (excursion and regular services)

Weisse Flotte *Schwerin*, Anlegestelle Schloss, Phone 0385/5811596,
Fax 0385/5811595

Swimming Pools and Sauna

Schwimmhalle, Wuppertaler Strasse, Grosser Dreesch, Phone 0385/375017;
Closed on Mondays, Tue/Fri 1400–2200, Wed 1400–1800, Thu 1400–2000,
Sat/Sun 1000–1800 Uhr, Sauna is available
Schwimmhalle Lankow, Fliederberg, Phone 0385/42188,
Tue/Thu 1400–1800, Wed/Fri 1400–2200, Sat 1000–1800, Sun 0900–1700

Theatre

Mecklenburgisches Staatstheater Schwerin, Am Alten Garten,
Phone 0385/5300-0, Fax 0385/5300-200;
Programme information: Phone 0385/5300-222
Visitor service: Tue–Fri 1000–1300 and 1400–1800 Uhr, Sat 1000–1300
Ticket counters: Phone 0385/5300-126 or 127 (reservation up to 14 days
ahead)
Venues: *Grosses Haus* and *Kammerbühne* at Theatergebäude at Old Gardens
TiK (Theater im Haus der Kultur*)*, Mecklenburgstr. 2, Phone 0385/559518
Puppets at *Haus »Thalia«*, Geschwister-Scholl-Str. 2

Youth Hostels

Jugendherberge Schwerin, Waldschulenweg 3, Phone 0385/213005
Jugendherberge Flessenow, 19067 Flessenow, Phone 03866/435

Zoo

Zoologischer Garten Schwerin, Waldschulenweg 1, Phone 0385/213000,
daily 0900–1700

Index

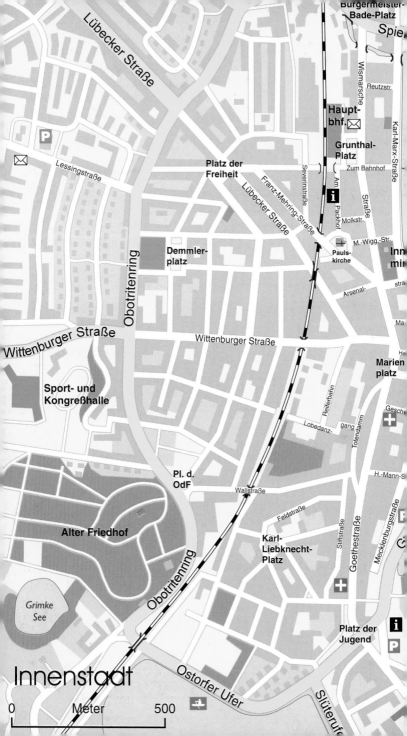